ISBN: 978-1-905540-70-9

Authors

Graeme Foreman and Andy Bradshaw

Contributing Authors

Richard Bailey, Craig Handford, Dave Harrison, Ian Stafford, Rod Thorpe

Technical Editors

Heather Moir and Anne Pankhurst

Coachwise editorial and design team

Christopher Stanners and Matthew Dodd

Cover photographs © The National Coaching Foundation and Action Images Limited/Reuters

Inner photographs © The National Coaching Foundation unless otherwise stated

sports coach UK
114 Cardigan Road
Headingley
Leeds LS6 3BJ

Tel: 0113-274 4802
Fax: 0113-275 5019
Email: coaching@sportscoachuk.org
Website: www.sportscoachuk.org

Patron: HRH The Princess Royal

Published on behalf of sports coach UK by

Coachwise Ltd
Chelsea Close
Off Amberley Road
Armley
Leeds LS12 4HP

Tel: 0113-231 1310
Fax: 0113-231 9606
Email: enquiries@coachwise.ltd.uk
Website: www.coachwise.ltd.uk

sports coach UK will ensure that it has professional and ethical values and that all its practices are inclusive and equitable.

90704:6

Contents

Foreword

I would like to propose three principles of child development that ought to be remembered by all coaches, teachers and policymakers:

- Children are not mini adults.

- Children are not mini adults.

- Children are not mini adults.

This point is trite and obvious, yet it has been repeatedly forgotten or ignored in sport.

We train infants as if they are fully developed adults, with adult physiology, motivations and systems. We talk about children's sporting 'careers'. We use children to help us realise our adult aspirations.

What is the result? Some children – often those who are initially most committed to sport – become burned out or are seriously injured. Others are turned off sport for life (let's not forget that most children in most countries do no regular sporting activity after leaving compulsory schooling). And even those who continue to play may have experiences that are less enjoyable and rewarding than they could be if we only remembered the three principles of child development.

The greatest achievement of long-term athlete development (LTAD), it seems to me, is that it has forced sports groups to acknowledge the relevance of a developmental perspective in sport. It has forced us to consider seriously the importance of children's physical, psychological and social development for their sports participation. Our understanding of child development is still emerging, and we can be sure that many of our assumptions will have to be adapted or overthrown. Much the same could be said for LTAD itself: it will have to evolve if it is to retain its relevance.

But one assumption seems to be quite secure: children's foundational experiences will have a massive influence on their later decisions to participate in sport. Fun and enjoyable early experiences are likely to nudge children towards a positive outcome in sport. And fun and enjoyment are the main reasons for children taking part in sport in the first place.

© Richard Bailey

This is an important book. It presents a wide range of information about children's development in an accessible way. It demonstrates through information and example the necessity of the fundamentals of movement and centrality of fun in sport. Coaches are encouraged to read it and apply its lessons in line with the Participant Development Model.

Richard Bailey PhD
Writer and consultant in education and sport

Introduction

> *Sport has an unmatched ability to mobilise and excite people in their millions. Sport matters to most people, but fewer of us play sport or are physically active on a regular basis.*
>
> **Department for Culture, Media and Sport, 2007**

Modern society is characterised by people becoming more sedentary, led by technology and with seemingly limited leisure and recreation time. For many, this statement is particularly relevant to their own lifestyle. Perhaps more importantly, it is also relevant to present-day children who are the targets of the fast food, television and video gaming industries. This resource considers and develops ideas that will introduce and encourage young children to adopt a healthy life in sport and physical activity. There has been much work recently on improving the delivery and processes involved in the journey 'from playground to podium', which has resulted in the establishment of an effective participant development model (Figure 1) that gives clear messages about the involvement of children in sport and physical activity.

The factors affecting lifestyle and physical activity levels within our society are all-encompassing and varied in nature, and include:

- the obesity 'epidemic'
- the increase in consumption of fast and convenience foods
- the growing popularity of computer games and consoles
- increased working hours
- less social and family time
- the breakdown of family values
- child protection concerns (the perception that it is not safe for children to play outside)
- the increase in the number of cars per household
- the decreasing number of 'playing areas'.

Any one or any combination of these factors can have a detrimental effect on a child's physical, mental and social development, as well as affecting his/her involvement in physical activity, sport and play.

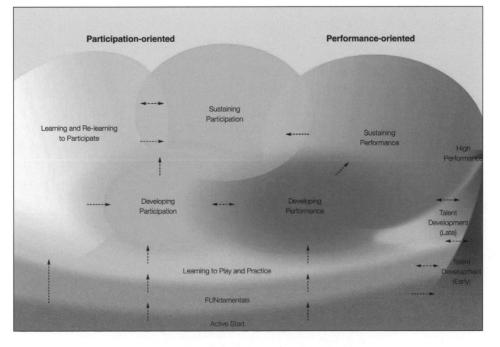

Figure 1: Participant Development Model

It is also widely accepted that many children have negative introductions to and experiences in sport and physical activity that can disengage them for life:

> I was never a fan of PE at school and I don't recall asking to be physically educated. It just seemed to happen and before I knew it my mum was sewing my initials on to the front of a gym bag and I was being forced to leap over a horsebox and perform a forward roll...
>
> If it had been up to me physical education would not have been on the curriculum...
>
> PE was just an opportunity for the fit kids to show up the fat kids...
>
> I was the last to get picked for any kind of sports and then even that usually resulted in a heated argument between the two team captains.
>
> And anyway, it didn't matter because whoever got me I'd still end up being put in a goal of some kind. It turned me off football for life.
>
> **Extracts from**
> **Peter Kay's autobiography**
> **The Sound of Laughter (2007)**

The objective of this resource is to help coaches, teachers and parents understand the importance of developing basic – fundamental – movement skills in young children. Every group of children and each individual child should have the opportunity to improve and increase the basic skills necessary to engage in physical activity, physical education and school sport. These basic skills are, essentially, the groundwork that underpins all movement and sports skills and, without them, the opportunities for developing and improving more specific skills in later years can become limited. The concept of FUNdamentals is the opportunity to teach and coach young children at the right level and in a way that is FUN, meaningful and engaging for them.

The principles of FUNdamentals are derived from, and are a part of, the concept of long-term athlete development (LTAD). LTAD is a staged model that provides coaches, teachers and parents with an understandable and realistic pathway for developing the capabilities (ie physical, psychological, technical, tactical, personal and lifestyle – see Figure 2) of young people. The model is important because it includes and outlines specific coaching principles and practices, which are relevant at the different stages.

Each stage of the LTAD model has a name that further serves to explain the key skills and capabilities children need to develop at that age and stage. FUNdamentals is the second stage of the LTAD model and is the subject of this resource.

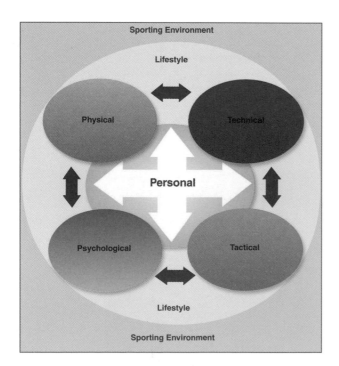

Figure 2: Participant capabilities

The FUNdamentals stage focuses on children between approximately six and nine years of age. This is a time when the activities and guidance young children experience often shape their perceptions of sport, their enjoyment of it and their desire to be involved at a later stage in their lives. As young people develop and mature, some may want nothing more from physical activity than an opportunity to socialise and stay healthy, others may gain real benefits and satisfaction from competing at club level, while a few have the desire (and ability) to progress and achieve at the highest levels. However, if the fundamental movement skills are not learnt at primary-school age, the variety of opportunities available in later years will almost certainly be more limited. Whatever path the individual takes in later life, in terms of sport and physical activity, the benefits of a good base in fundamental movement skills cannot be overstated:

> *The critical, fundamental phase is often overlooked by coaches, teachers and parents, who focus on competition and winning rather than the acquisition of basic skills and fitness.*
>
> **Balyi, 2001**

> *It is now critical that schools, communities and parents are able to offer activity experiences that are not only fun, safe and worthwhile, but which also help children develop a solid foundation for a lifetime of physical activity.*
>
> **Jess, 2004**

The discussion and quotes above set the context for the importance of this *Introduction to the FUNdamentals of Movement* resource and its accompanying workshop. Both support the need for further learning in the area of introducing and developing fundamental movement skills with young children. The resource is in two sections and is aimed at coaches, teachers and parents.

Section One aims to provide the background information of FUNdamentals, while **Section Two** gives practical ideas to help coaches, teachers and parents

understand the 'what' and 'how' of providing young children with an enjoyable and challenging introduction to 'physical literacy'[1].

The contents of this resource include:

* a detailed explanation of the LTAD model

* an explanation of the rationale behind the FUNdamentals of Movement and the importance of FUNdamentals as a building block for physical skill development

* an introduction to the physical and mental/emotional abilities of young children

* an analysis of the coaching skills needed to work with young children

* an overview of FUNdamentals in the bigger picture of British sport

* a detailed analysis of the FUNdamental skills of balance, coordination and agility

* practical ideas and guidance on how to deliver FUNdamentals effectively

* information on future learning.

[1] Physical literacy refers to the acquisition of, and the ability to learn and use, a wide variety of basic physical skills, such as agility, balance, coordination, running, jumping and throwing.

Section One

The Background to the FUNdamentals of Movement

Traditionally, sport has played a valuable role in society in terms of 'sport for sport's sake'. The intrinsic value of participating in sport is generally accepted, although that value has, perhaps, been less well supported by research evidence. Currently, sport is widely used as a key vehicle for the promotion of positive social change, but for this to be truly effective, coaches and teachers must ensure children and young people are given every opportunity to achieve their ambitions and fulfil their potential. Through experiencing achievement, children and young people develop greater confidence and self-esteem.

A number of coaches might share the concerns voiced by many teachers: that their role has changed subtly over time into more 'social work' rather than the promotion of their sport. Although sport is perceived to be a very useful tool in addressing many social issues, such as health and social inclusion, the primary role of a coach working with children and young people should still be **the improvement of participation and performance in sport**. In providing a developmentally appropriate environment in which children and young people can learn and develop sport-related skills, coaches will be increasing their chances of experiencing achievement, with all the attendant social and psychological benefits that may bring. There is no doubt sport has the potential to provide rewarding and fulfilling experiences that can enhance positive individual development, but only if it is presented and structured appropriately. This underlines the importance of one key aspect of The UK Coaching Framework vision: having **skilled coaches working to support participants at all levels and stages of their development**. However, as discussed in the **Introduction**, the work undertaken during the early stages of involvement in sport is particularly crucial.

Long-term Athlete Development (LTAD)

LTAD is a concept that has helped focus attention more sharply on key, common principles of athlete or player development. It has proved to be a very useful driver for change within many governing bodies of sport and national agencies in the UK. It has led to an overall review of what is considered good practice in long-term

planning for children's and young people's development **in** and **through** sport. As an example, many governing bodies and agencies have now started to examine their existing competitive structures and training practices, and review how young people are developed in sport. Typically, young people take part in sport into their early teens and then drop out shortly afterwards. A variety of reasons have been suggested for this, but there is a strong possibility that this drop out may be related to the way young people are developed from the outset. Clearly, a logical, progressive approach to developing young people in sport is necessary, whatever their aspirations may be.

LTAD is a long-term approach to maximising individual potential and involvement in sport. For many years, high-quality coaches have been working with high-level performers, but one of the central messages to emerge from LTAD is the importance of having high-quality coaches working with children and young people during the early stages of their development in sport. A skilled coach has to understand and account for the different needs and motivations of children and young people as they progress through the various stages and levels of participation and performance.

Coaches should be aware that the principles and guidelines set out in this resource are central to an evolving and flexible approach to developing sporting abilities. These principles and guidelines should not be seen as rigid rules – **good coaches coach people**! If a real participant-centred coaching system is to be developed, then training, preparation, competition and recovery programmes must account for individual differences.

It is also important to understand that LTAD is **not**:

• new

• the only model

• set in stone

• to be implemented without due thought to individuals and the nature and culture of different sports.

© Richard Heathcote Livepic/Action Images Limited

The Key Principles of the LTAD Model

The principles listed below are important in understanding the concept of the LTAD model. They include some that are beyond the scope of this resource as they are outside the FUNdamentals stage of

development, but it is nonetheless important for coaches, teachers and parents to understand the all-embracing aspects of the model.

• The nature of growing children and their stage of development (physical, cognitive, social and emotional) must be a central consideration when planning and implementing coaching programmes.

• The importance of FUNdamentals skills and the physical literacy gained during a child's early sport experiences to subsequent development must be understood.

• Differences in the nature of sports, whether or not they require young people to specialise in them at an early age or later, are key in determining training and competition programmes.

• Particular attention should be paid to sensitive periods (so-called 'windows of trainability') that appear at different times during the process of maturation. If these sensitive periods are fully appreciated and exploited, the training effect will be optimal and help significantly in realising true potential.

• The review of programmes of training and competition for young athletes might involve more innovative and creative thinking from coaches, as well as the restructuring of competitive experiences. Coaches are challenged to consider what they can do and what they can influence.

• It is necessary to involve a whole range of significant other people, such as parents, teachers, administrators, fixture secretaries and officials, in order to produce an integrated and progressive sport experience for young people.

• The key requirement is to strive for 'system integration', or 'pulling it all together' for the athlete, in terms of sport experience in schools and clubs, coaching programmes, coach education, competitive structures and appropriate support systems.

• The commitment to continuous improvement is essential. Any LTAD model should reflect good coaching practice in terms of being constantly reviewed and improved in the light of research evidence and changing environments.

• For potential to be realised, it can take approximately 10 years of extensive and progressive practice to really excel.

Table 1: The stages of the LTAD model

Early-specialisation Sports	Late-specialisation Sports
1 Active Start	1 Active Start (up to 6 years)
2 FUNdamentals	2 FUNdamentals (girls 6–8 years; boys 6–9 years)
3 Training to Train	3 Learning to Play and Practice (girls 8–11 years; boys 9–12 years)
4 Training to Compete	4 Training to Train (girls 11–15 years; boys 12–16 years)
5 Training to Win	5 Training to Compete (girls 15–17 years; boys 16–18 years)
6 Retaining	6 Training to Win (girls 17+; boys 18+)
	7 Retaining (varies depending on individual and sport)

Adapted from Stafford and Balyi (2005)

The Stages of the LTAD Model

The stages of the current LTAD model are set out in Table 1 above. The stages differ depending on whether the sport is an early- or late-specialisation sport. Although age ranges are shown, coaches should remember that it is the actual developmental age of the young person that is key to planning and implementing effective coaching programmes.

Although this resource is concerned primarily with FUNdamentals, it is important for coaches, teachers and parents to know and understand the features of the preceding and following stages of the LTAD model. In developing the UK-wide Participant Development Model, the first three stages for late-specialisation sports have recently been reviewed and are described below. This description also helps coaches, teachers and parents understand the stages of development preceding and following the FUNdamentals stage.

1   **Active Start (up to six years of age)**. The aim of this stage is to develop good physical activity habits early by focusing on fun, playful games, daily physical activity and basic movement skills. This concept is reinforced in the coaching literature:

> *A playful environment during the early years of a child's involvement in sport may explain the early learning and exceptional motivation of expert athletes because it appears to lead to subsequent learning and involvement in deliberate practice.*
>
> **Côté et al, 2003**

(Deliberate practice is more appropriate and necessary for older athletes at a more advanced stage of their development. This is because it involves lengthy and repetitive practice with no immediate reward – a structure and practice that is not fun for young children.)

2   **FUNdamentals (girls 6–8 years; boys 6–9 years)**. At this stage, the aim is to initiate more formalised and structured movement education. This is achieved through fun activities that develop both movement and more general skills while introducing children to the basic spirit/ethics of sport at the same time. At this stage, the focus is on developing the FUNdamentals of Movement ABCs – agility, balance, coordination and speed.

3   **Learning to Play and Practice (girls 8–11 years; boys 9–12 years)**. This stage aims to provide children with a wide range of appropriate and basic sport skills that develop the necessary levels of competence and confidence to progress their development in sport. Early diversification is encouraged in order for children to develop a broad range of sport skills. The emphasis is clearly on skill development. To ensure children have the opportunity to apply their developing skills and stay motivated, competitive events such as festival participation are recommended. At this stage, it is important that the balance between training and developing skills and formalised competition is in favour of skill development. The ratio of training to competition should be approx 80:20. Again, the key message is reinforced in the coaching literature:

> *Pre-adolescent athletes have not yet learned how to engage in task persistence, how to delay gratification, or how to be self-controlled; the focus of training for athletes of this age should be on learning basic cognitive and motor skills through deliberate play activities.*
>
> **Côté et al, 2003**

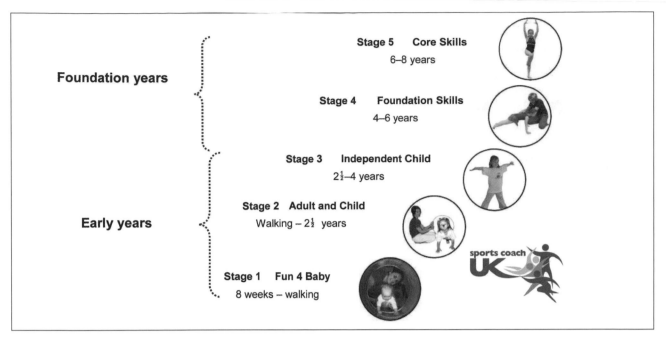

Figure 3: Pathway of FUNdamental movement stages

Figure 3 shows the progressive pathway for FUNdamentals in a diagram format. It also shows the importance of adults in the early years and the increasing independence of the child.

Summary

The LTAD model arose from a need to rationalise the current sport system in the UK by putting the participant at the centre of the system. The model is a pathway and a simple, common sense approach to developing young people in sport. In the first three stages that include the FUNdamentals, the focus of coaching should be on process goals and not the performance outcome. LTAD alerts coaches to the dangers of young people specialising too early, by identifying the shortcomings that may occur if too much emphasis is placed on formal competition in the early stages. The model has both talent development and improving participation dimensions and applications. It advocates 'evolution, not revolution'!

Sport has the potential to influence the lives of children, adults, communities and nations, but only if it is structured, presented well and meets the needs of young people. Coaches are without a doubt key in ensuring that crucial early experiences set the foundation for a lifelong involvement in sport.

The Background to FUNdamentals

Understanding Child Development

Children progress through two key processes as they grow and develop:

1   physical development

2   mental and emotional development.

Coaches need to understand the processes of both and the impact each has on coaching practice.

Observation Point for the Coach

It would be worthwhile for a coach to spend time observing both children and adults moving and playing games in order to appreciate the differences between them. By first observing a coaching session or a physical education session for children in the FUNdamentals age group (6–9-year-olds) and then watching adults take part in sport, the coach can easily identify a number of key differences and recognise skills that underpin fundamental movement skills. A simple comparison of the different physiques of children and adults, the different ways in which they move and the activities that children find challenging and adults find easy, should give coaches much food for thought.

1 The Process of Physical Development

The differences in physical growth and development can be seen in everyday life. People differ in terms of their height, weight and the length of their arms and legs. They also differ in their fitness and in their ability to move and perform physical skills.

Probably the most obvious and, by far, the most important thing to learn from this observation, is the great differences between the children and the adults:

Children are not simply small adults. Indeed, they differ from adults qualitatively as well as quantitatively.

Sharp, 1991

With this in mind, it simply does not make sense to coach children with scaled-down versions of adult methods and practices as children's and adults' experiences, as well as their learning and skills abilities, are so different. To maximise learning and achievement for children, the coach needs to recognise the different ways children respond to sporting challenges and adapt the coaching accordingly.

The different needs of children are the reason for, and the basis of, the FUNdamentals approach to coaching. Lifelong physical activity is built on a strong foundation of basic skills, relevant experiences and enjoyment. Without these, inactive children can become inactive adults. In the past, sports coaching has been bedevilled by the well-meaning, but ultimately harmful effects of enforcing adult expectations, abilities and practices on still-developing children. For example, small children playing in large teams with unsuitable equipment, in huge playing areas, to adult-designed rules are a recipe for frustration and failure. Inappropriate activities like these may well contribute to children becoming progressively disillusioned with sport, and result in them dropping out altogether.

In addition, inappropriate coaching methods can result in children being overtrained. Overtraining occurs when the amount and intensity of training is greater than the person's capacity to recover. When this happens, the athlete ceases to make progress and performance levels can start to regress. Children are also vulnerable to injury.

Coaches should never forget that children are not small versions of adults and require child-specific coaching.

Coaches should also think about what children enjoy doing a great deal of the time. Most of them play. Play for a young child is a very important way of learning physical and social skills and, as playing takes up a great deal of children's waking hours, it is the principle way in which they find out about their bodies and their movement. So, coaching young children through play would be very meaningful and productive (see pages 17–18 for further information).

The stages of physical growth and development

While the basic pattern of physical growth is similar for everyone, there can be a great deal of variation between individuals in terms of the rate and timing of growth. The normal reference point for assessing the stage of development is chronological age. However, this is a poor point of reference due to the different rates of growth in different individuals. There can be huge differences in all the physical measures of height, weight and arm/leg length, even between children born on the same day. Remember, biology does not celebrate birthdays!

Observation Point for the Coach

An easy way for coaches to see the variation in growth between different children of the same age is to take a small group of 10- or 11-year-old boys and girls and line them up next to each other. (It is important that both boys and girls are represented for reasons explained later.) A variation in height will be obvious. Some of the group will be quite tall and gangly, while others will be short and squat. Some may be showing the early signs of puberty, but others will still look like very young children.

A group of children of this age will be a mixture of prepubescent and pubescent children, and so there will be visible differences in physique and physical ability.

The basic pattern of physical growth over the stages of LTAD is:

1   a period of rapid growth during early childhood (until about seven years of age)

followed by

2   steady development during the later childhood: 8–11/12 (or until the start of puberty)

followed by

3   another period of rapid growth during puberty until the growth spurt is completed

and then

4   a slow increase in growth until adult stature is reached.

There is a well-defined growth spurt during adolescence. This is when children experience a marked increase in both physical stature and weight. Some children, but not all, also undergo a less obvious growth spurt at the end of their first phase of rapid growth at around six or seven years of age. Despite the general pattern of growth, all coaches will know that there will be a great deal of variation within and between each group of children. One of the reasons for this is gender. Boys and girls follow a similar pattern of growth in childhood, but there are differences in both the timing and degree of change as they get older. Gender differences are normally insignificant before adolescence. However, girls normally enter puberty up to two years earlier than boys and, consequently, their growth spurt finishes earlier. A few girls reach puberty as early as seven years of age, but most do so between 10 and 12 years of age. Boys, on average, begin their growth spurt at around 12–14 years of age. So, in the group of 10- and 11-year-olds discussed earlier, the fact that both boys and girls were included will contribute to the variation in height.

Coaches will also understand that children are not simply getting taller and heavier throughout the growth spurt, but the proportions of their body are changing as well. Toddlers have relatively large heads in proportion to the rest of their body and relatively short legs and arms.

The verb 'to toddle' means to walk with an unsteady action, and it is hardly surprising that young children walk like this because they have a high centre of gravity and poor stability as a result.

As children grow and mature, their body shape changes; the head becomes less and less dominant and the body becomes more 'bottom heavy'. This means the child becomes more stable because the centre of gravity is lower. When the principles of balance are discussed on page 33, the gradual change in the centre of gravity for children will be important.

Physical activity will, in general, make a positive contribution to children's physical development. There is a great deal of evidence that regular exercise can strengthen children's bones. The stop-start movements associated with most sports will help muscular development, and the weight-bearing aspects of different games seem to contribute to the growth of wider, stronger bones. However, coaches should understand that because children's bones are still growing and developing and their skeletons are slowly changing from quite soft cartilage to the more rigid bone of adulthood, children are susceptible to injury. The major areas of growth are the long bones of the arms and legs. Bone develops from the centre outwards and also at each end of the bone. These areas are the 'weak link' in children's limbs because the relative 'softness' of the cartilage is not designed to withstand very strong muscular action. Therefore, activities such as landing from a height, explosive starts, deep knee bends and repetitive bouncing can be harmful to a child's soft, still-forming frame.

Physical development and movement skills

As children's bodies develop and mature, their movement skills should improve. Babies start to explore their environments through movement almost from the time they are born. Through a combination of play, imitation and trial and error, children acquire an increasingly sophisticated and specialised set of movement skills, which help them face the physical challenges presented to them during life.

Some researchers believe that the period from childhood to puberty offers a 'sensitive period' for developing basic movements and skills and the LTAD model supports this concept. These sensitive periods are times when children find learning certain skills very easy and make progress very rapidly. For example, the period between the ages of eight and 12 is seen as a sensitive period when children can make rapid progress in learning sport (motor) skills. This becomes clear in the realisation that this is a period of relatively slow growth and so the body is able to progress such skills rapidly.

Other researchers go further, arguing that the period of childhood is so critical for skill learning that if children do not develop skills during this period, they will find the process harder in later life and are unlikely to reach their full potential.

It is probably fair to say that some of the evidence on these sensitive periods is unclear, partly because it is very difficult to imagine an ethical experiment in which young children are deliberately deprived of the opportunity to learn to move! However, many coaches will know from experience that children do make rapid progress in different activities at different stages in their lives. They can also recognise teenagers who have poor coordination and movement skills and find sport very difficult.

Evidently, childhood is a pivotal period in the development of physical movement skills and there is a set of patterns that runs parallel with children's physical growth, relating to different aspects of physical development. There is some variation in the ages at which children develop specific skills, simply because of the differing rates and times of growth between individuals. However, as with growth and development, the basic patterns seem universal.

Patterns of physical development

A number of patterns form the development of movement skills in young children, which are discussed in detail below and are helpful for coaches concerned with the development of fundamental movement skills in young children.

1 The general to specific pattern

The development of movement skills follows a pattern of learning that progresses from basic and generic movement to increasingly specific and specialised actions. In part, this is a process of children acquiring and refining actions as they learn to perform skills with greater control, fluency and precision. So, for example, a young child might start by kicking a ball and, once that basic action becomes established, progress to kicking for distance or accuracy. Later still, the child progresses to moving the ball in specific directions with different techniques.

In general terms, up to the age of seven, children are laying the foundations of a lifetime of movement. They are (or should be) exploring and extending their capabilities in a wide range of fundamental movement skills. The generic movement skills associated with this stage are those concerned with:

- locomotion (running, walking, leaping, jumping, skipping)

- manipulation (holding, throwing, kicking, catching, rolling)

- balance (bending, stretching, twisting, turning, stopping).

At this age, the key is the diversity of experience over time, rather than the depth of it. The child needs to experience as many skills as possible. Highly technical and specific instruction is usually inappropriate because it is important for the child to develop generic skills. In addition, the years up to seven are often characterised by quite rapid physical growth so specialised skills will be difficult to learn for the simple reason that the body is always changing. However, after this age, and until puberty begins, the rate of physical growth slows down

and the child is much better able to acquire more specialised skills.

The period from seven years of age until puberty is sometimes called the 'skill-hungry years'. Children should already have a basic repertoire of fundamental movement skills and are now ready to develop more specialised skills for more specific situations. They do this by combining, refining and elaborating their general skills in new contexts and by seeking out (or being given) new challenges and opportunities to increase the range and quality of their movements.

One way in which children's skills and understanding are developed between the ages of eight/nine and 11/12 is through being involved in more structured activities. Younger children thrive on simple games, with minimal rules and basic movement skills. As they get older, children are ready for games and activities with greater structure, more complex rules and a greater variety of roles.

Most children in the FUNdamentals stage are eager to extend their range of skills. Motivation is rarely a problem for the coach. Children become progressively more able to perform specialised actions associated with different sports, dance and games when they can practise fundamental movement skills in new situations and combinations.

© Action Images Limited/Reuters

2   The proximal to distal pattern

Children also develop movement skills from the centre of their bodies outwards, from near to far (ie from proximal to distal). Underpinning this pattern of development is the principle that the head and trunk develop before the arms and legs, and the arms and legs before the fingers and toes. This means that young children learn to control their heads and bodies before they acquire control of their limbs. When they are capable of controlling their arms and legs, they then begin to learn the finer, more detailed movements of the hands and feet.

3   The unilateral to bilateral pattern

A parallel pattern that relates closely to the proximal to distal pattern of development is that of the changing and progressive organisation of different parts of the body, especially the limbs. The child will progress from using one arm or leg (unilateral) to being able to combine and coordinate both limbs together (bilateral). This is **coordination** and it is a very visible (and necessary) element of children's development, especially in playing different games or in dance. An important variation of the unilateral to bilateral pattern is contralateral coordination, by which children are able to undertake physical activities with opposite arms and legs. Walking is an example of contralateral coordination because it combines the opposite foot to the leading hand. Sport has numerous instances of this type of action, such as a bowling action in cricket and the front crawl in swimming.

Physical development and coaching practice

Between the ages of five and 12, children will learn a remarkable range of physical skills. Their bodies will develop and change. For most of them, physical activity and games are an important element of their lives. The quality of the experiences in learning skills can leave a legacy lasting many years. Sports coaching can play a valuable role by building on children's natural drive to play and learn new skills, but this coaching must be based on a child-centred approach and link closely to children's physical abilities as they grow and develop.

It is important to consider the following implications for coaching practice, in the light of children's growth and development:

1   Movements and practices that regularly occur in adult coaching sessions are unlikely to be suitable for children. Children's bodies are immature and still growing and developing. All activities should relate to the ages and stages of the children.

2   Not all activities will be appropriate for every child, even those of the same age. Since chronological age is a poor indicator of physical maturity, the coach should plan tasks that are adaptable and open-ended. This is especially the case around the beginning of puberty, when children can have very different physiques and abilities. Activities and challenges will need to be adapted to maximise learning and minimise the risk of injury or frustration.

3   Patience on the part of the coach will be essential, as rapid growth spurts can mean that a young person can become temporarily unable to perform a skill that once was easy. Some might find themselves moving in clumsy or ungainly ways. For children who define themselves in terms of their sporting ability, this apparent reduction of skill can be very upsetting. They need reassurance that their growing body is developing in its own way and to its own timetable – and that the skill level will return!

Having considered the physical development of children, especially in the first three stages of LTAD, it is also important to understand their psychological and social development.

Summary of patterns of physical development

For coaches, the implications of these patterns will be clear and make sense, even if, on occasions, they are forgotten. Young children should play running and chasing games that involve their whole body before they play throwing and catching games that involve the manipulation of balls. Similarly, they should learn to throw before they learn the 'leg break' bowling action in cricket. They should also get opportunities to practise skills with single limbs before coordinating both together, or even in opposition to each other.

Underpinning these patterns of development is the basic concept that young children need to progress from simple movement skills to more complex ones. If children have repeated difficulties performing skills, the coach should look for ways to simplify the task and so increase the likelihood of success. If children do not seem ready for specialist skills, they will benefit from more experience of the basics. If they struggle with manipulating balls or other equipment, encourage them to bring the ball or equipment closer to their bodies, or just practise controlling it on one side of their body or with both hands together. The key message is that at the heart of FUNdamentals is fun and progress.

2 The Process of Psychological and Social Development

Developing fundamental movement skills in young children is only one of the concerns for coaches working with this group. The second major consideration for coaches is to understand the development of psychological and social skills in young children.

The characteristics of young children are very different and change as they develop. They:

- are interested in new things and inquisitive, but can quickly become bored with repetition

- lose confidence quickly if they do not succeed in a task

- do not understand why they cannot perform a task, especially if they feel they are trying hard

- learn many skills by copying others

- learn skills through play activities with their peer group or parents

- have little concept of time

- find it hard to understand the concepts of winning and losing

- can usually only concentrate for short periods of time

- get better at cooperating with other children in different size groups as they get older

- like being with their friends

- enjoy being with adults whom they like and who make things fun.

The importance of understanding the psychological and social development of young children cannot be overstated because it impacts on everything they do and how they are coached. For example, to improve basic movement skills means that the child will have to repeat them many times. Psychologically, repetition is boring for a child. So the coach needs to find different and fun ways of doing the same thing. One way could be to encourage children to play and practise on their own or with their friends to help them to improve through repetition.

As another example, for the child to want to continue with an activity, confidence through success (especially for girls) is crucial. This means that physical skills must be developed in 'small steps' so that success is possible.

This concept of understanding the mental, emotional and social abilities of children raises basic issues for coaches. In the first three stages of LTAD especially, the coaching practice must 'match' the needs of the

children. If it does not, it is quite possible that some of them will choose not to continue.

The stress on the 'fun' in FUNdamentals and the modification of the original LTAD models to include Learning to Play and Practice as the third stage of the model indicate that there is a commitment to teaching young children movement and sport skills in a way that is appropriate to their age.

Meeting the Needs of Children at the FUNdamentals Stage

The following coaching points for FUNdamentals come from an understanding of the psychological and social needs of young children:

1   Coaches must be sensitive to the motivation young children feel from being coached in a fun way, and understand how this helps develop the attitudes that will ensure continued participation.

2   When children learn an activity (such as throwing) with children who can already do it, they are often motivated to improve. Most will get better without any direct input from the coach. This also illustrates the importance of coaching often being best achieved through 'play'. Play and fun are the same thing to young children.

3   Since young children learn by copying and being with their friends, the social organisation of any coaching session is important to consider. Observational learning is very powerful so structuring a session so children can see others and compare themselves in an informal way can be very useful.

4   At times, however, providing ways in which children can 'have a go' without others watching is equally important, especially for the less able and less confident. This could be achieved by having a circuit of different fun activities the children can move around. The fact that some children move away from traditional team games when they reach 10–12 years of age may be because they have been offered no way of avoiding direct comparison and/or 'intense' competition. Learning may best be achieved if, on occasions, children are encouraged to take part in coaching sessions with structured play situations, in which the equipment and environment encourage the use of skills needed for the sport or activity, but where the children are left to determine their own activity.

5   Coaches need to beware of trying to help children too much by using very direct (and often detailed)

approaches. In this sense, the traditional coaching approach may have been less than helpful, especially for young children. The UK Coaching Certificate (UKCC), in looking far more at **how** people learn, and only then considering how coaching helps these processes, has highlighted certain key elements. So coaching practice that reflects the psychological and social skills and abilities in young children, rather than the requirement of the sport, is far more appropriate and relevant.

6   Research has shown children develop and improve a large number of social (and movement) skills through play that is unsupervised and where they have created the 'rules' – but only if they are given the chance and have confidence to do so. Increasingly, children have more opportunities for coaching than, say, 50 years ago, but they also have fewer opportunities for play away from adult supervision. There are social reasons for this, the greatest being the perceived danger of allowing youngsters to 'play out'. The outcome of this is that many physical experiences for children tend to be in adult-controlled environments.

7   Adults have expectations of **rapid** improvement in the controlled coaching environment, especially if the parents are paying for coaching. While success is a major motivator for young children and is important for building confidence and self-esteem, easy and rapid improvements can become associated with the skills of the coach, rather than with the efforts of the learner.

8   When working with young children, there are sometimes conflicting considerations for coaches. First is the importance of meeting the present needs of the child to develop skills and abilities. Second is the need to prepare the child for a future as an active adult. Often, these two considerations coincide because the child who enjoys and is successful in a sport is more likely to continue in that sport. This may seem obvious, but in reality and from research, many talented young people do not go on to be successful adults in their chosen sport, although they may, of course, enjoy physical activity.

9   LTAD recognises the need for long-term development. The stages of the model reflect child development and the physical, mental, emotional and social skills and abilities that are possible to develop in young children at each stage. To gain the most benefit from LTAD, coaches need to look more carefully at the needs of each child and consider more carefully the way they coach.

Child Development and Task Progression

This section of the resource has discussed the development of physical, psychological and social skills in children. Figure 4 summarises the progressive development children will make in physical, sensory and social skills, and indicates how different tasks should be progressed in line with the child's development:

1   proximal → distal
2   unilateral → bilateral → contralateral
3   kinaesthetic → visual
4   single senses → multiple senses
5   egocentric → social.

All the physical and learning preference skills are encompassed within the progression from balance to coordination to agility and will apply to every child.

As in the development of physical skills, different children will progress at different rates in other areas shown on the graph. Some will develop social skills quickly while, for others, sensory skills might be learnt faster.

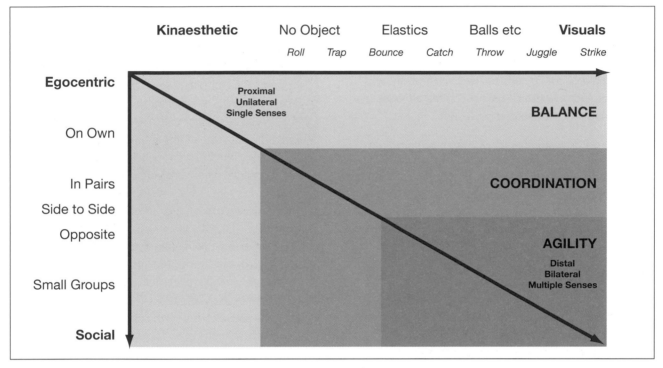

Figure 4: Child development task progression graph

Coaching Skills for the Active Start, FUNdamentals and Learning to Play and Practice Stages of LTAD

Understanding the processes of physical, psychological and social development in young children makes it possible to link coaching skills to the Active Start, FUNdamentals and Learning to Play and Practice stages of LTAD.

It is clear that a child's stage of development is the key focus at every stage of the LTAD model. The discussion in the Introduction of this resource highlighted the fact that the FUNdamentals stage is key because it provides an opportunity to teach and develop the physical and movement skills required to participate in any form of sport, play or physical activity throughout life. At the same time, it is also of vital importance that society addresses the issues of physical inactivity and imbalanced lifestyles, which are coming to dominate modern-day life.

For coaches to understand the importance of FUNdamentals, it is essential they understand the developmental stage that precedes it – Active Start – and that which follows – Learning to Play and Practice.

Stage 1: Active Start
(pre-school experience up to six years of age)

This is the stage of child development where movement experiences are critical because they set the pattern for future development. Understandably, many would argue that 'coaching', in the manner by which the practice is normally understood, is inappropriate for pre-school children. This is because the child's understanding of language is less well developed and concepts that involve consequence are not well formed at this age so explanations of what to do are often meaningless. However, visual (or, with visually impaired children, tactile) stimulation is relevant for this age group. For example, young children of this age watch and copy what other children do and they also want to move and be active. They may climb on to a chair or kick a ball because an older sister or brother did so, often saying 'I want a go', having seen what another child is doing. Coaches should realise how much imitative behaviour occurs at this age and how they can use it in their coaching by providing play opportunities in which, for example, younger children can copy older ones. The coach's role should then be to interject and to encourage or help as required.

Even at this age, interaction with others is often a key element of a child's enjoyment of a coaching session. As an example, on leaving a beginner gymnastics session, a four-year-old girl was asked by her mother how the session went. The girl's reply was 'Millie wasn't there'. This illustrates that while coaches may be working on

improving movement, perceptual decision making and social skills, for the child, other things are also important. Social interaction and being with friends is an important reason why young children take part in activity and this has implications for the organisation of the session.

The coaching of young children is criticised at times because the real reasons why children take part are sometimes forgotten. In addition, the use of rewards by the coach to recognise success in different activities becomes more important than children playing by themselves.

Stage 2: FUNdamentals
(6–8/6–9 years of age)

Recently, one of the most significant changes in the coaching of early primary-school-age children has been the acceptance by most sports of the need to address the FUNdamentals of Movement, rather than concentrating on the technical demands of the sport. Few would argue with the idea that agility, balance, coordination and speed are vital to performance in sport.

Early primary-school-age children are not able to assess their own abilities with any accuracy. In the previous section, it was mentioned that children think that if they try harder, they will succeed. However, by the time they finish primary school, most children have well-formed views of their ability – it is not unusual for a child of 10 to say 'I am no good at sport'.

From a coaching viewpoint, the important consideration is to motivate the child to want to take part in physical activity. However, those children who are not succeeding and improving could lose confidence rapidly in activities that stress agility, balance and coordination. This situation is made worse by the fact that, to improve the ABCs or basic skills over time, they must be repeated and practised so coaching has to be fun. Coaches also know that the development of the ABCs will give children more opportunities later in life, but young children do not understand the concept of the future – they live in the present!

In the previous section (page 14), it was emphasised that coaching practice at the FUNdamentals stage must be relevant to the needs of the children. Two key issues are repeated here:

- 'Deliberate' and 'free' play (for all ability levels) should stimulate and practise different ABCs and movement skills both in and beyond the session.

- Different, fun and interesting ways of doing the same thing must be found in order for the children to succeed and develop confidence.

The words **fun** and **enjoyment** are often used to describe physical activity for young children. For coaches, the important question is: what makes a session fun and/or enjoyable for the child?

Most research seems to agree that for a child:

- feeling competent and successful

- being able to be part of the group and interacting with others

- experiencing excitement and even a little anxiety

all contribute to enjoyment and having fun.

Many adults learnt the physical ABCs and movement skills through traditional children's games, which develop ABCs and are fun and enjoyable for children and could easily be used by coaches. Consider the balance, agility and coordination needed to play hopscotch. 'What's the time, Mr Wolf?' involves children moving forward, but having to 'freeze' suddenly in a balanced position. The child playing 'Mr Wolf' has to use peripheral vision to catch someone moving. Kicking a ball involves balancing on one leg while swinging the other – two basic skills. Perceptual judgements and dodging skills are involved in tag games. Dodging, itself, involves quite sophisticated dynamic balance skills. The excitement (almost the 'fear') when children realise they are about to be tagged simply adds the fun element to developing such skills.

(Recently, the original LTAD model has been developed to include perceptual skills because, just as the physical skills should be challenged, so should perception and decision making.)

Stage 3: Learning to Play and Practice
(8/9–11/12 years of age)

By this stage, youngsters are beginning to assess their own ability more accurately, and the concept of being 'no good' occurring to them becomes a real possibility.

This stage, insensitively handled, should also be viewed as the first point of a possible lapse in participation.

The Learning to Play and Practice stage stresses the development of a range of basic sports skills, which will advance competence and confidence in sport. A major advantage, in terms of coaching practice, is not to align skills too closely to a given sport at any one time. The coach can match skill demands to the ability of the children, especially when equipment is used. When facing different challenges, children are given a greater chance of progress in a number of areas. Often, when they grasp the first steps of learning different skills (if the skill is well matched to their ability), children show rapid improvement. Many are still not ready to persist in a task for long enough to improve their skills, but they will go back to a game or activity many times if it is fun. Again, play activities are important, but at this stage, the progression of skill moves from 'free' play to 'deliberate' play. Children can organise games that test their abilities and modify the game as they play.

Competition, in the form of festivals, is meaningful, fun and enjoyable for many children. However, coaches should be aware that not all children enjoy competition, particularly if their lack of ability is exposed. Peer opinion at this age is important, and while competition can increase excitement and interest, it should be remembered that it is an adult concept and is different for children. For some, it can be stressful, and some will choose not to take part.

Using a 'games for understanding'/'games sense' approach will help develop cognitive understanding, as well as basic skills, and so provide more opportunities for success and progress. Children at this age can achieve success in a number of ways, which suit them as individuals (Whitehead, 1993). For example, success could be showing ability, task mastery, gaining social approval, winning, finally achieving, or being a team member. A major role for the coach is to structure coaching sessions to ensure children achieve success in a way that meets their individual needs. The organised social interaction can, if well managed, maximise their need to be part of the group.

Summary

This section has highlighted the key issues for coaching practice throughout the first three stages of LTAD. The importance of play, fun and enjoyment as the means of learning and continuing physical activity outside of coaching sessions has been highlighted.

The coaching session should only be part of a child's general learning environment at all three of these stages.

Encouraging deliberate and free play helps children:

- develop skills by repetition in a fun and enjoyable way

- break the dependence on the coach for participation and learning

- prepare for transfer into the teenage years when, in some cases, adults become less influential and, in the case of 'performance' athletes/players, considerable personal motivation will be necessary.

However, a major issue in using play-like activities, where the coach is continually developing situations that challenge the skills of the children, is that parents will be expecting coaches to be 'showing and telling' the children what to do. The more coaches say (often, the more they find fault), the more they encourage and thus the better the parents think they coach. The fact that, at the football club, the younger children are playing tag games and not being shown a sport-specific technique may be questioned.

Educating parents about FUNdamentals is crucial so they understand the importance of:

- preparing children for the future, while doing activities that they enjoy

- their own role in supervising deliberate play and encouraging free-play activities with their children, at home or in the park

- enabling youngsters to play and practise without relying on the coach.

How FUNdamentals Fits into the Bigger Picture

This section highlights the roles of a number of agencies involved in developing sports and physical activity programmes for children. It explains their approaches to the development of FUNdamentals. The purpose is to give the 'bigger picture' and show how the different agencies are working together.

1 Youth Sport Trust

Youth Sport Trust has worked hard over recent years to develop school sport through school sport partnerships (SSPs). The SSPs comprise partnership development managers, school sport coordinators, primary link teachers and competition managers. The development of this structure has led to improved quality provision of school sport, the development of FUNdamental and multi-skill clubs, and FUNdamental and multi-skill festivals. This has improved the development link from schools to local sports clubs in order to enhance the overall sport-participation framework.

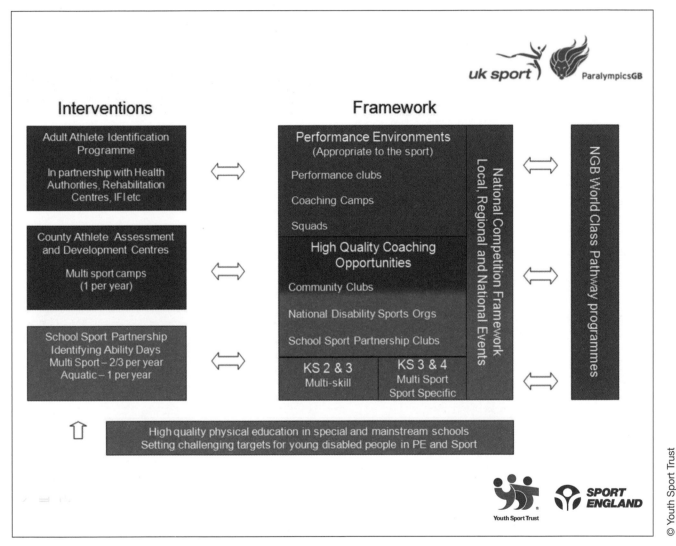

Figure 5: The playground to podium framework

Figure 5 depicts a framework for the development of FUNdamentals within schools, clubs and governing bodies. FUNdamentals should be developed in schools from Key Stage 2 onwards. Therefore, it is important for schools to build and interpret FUNdamentals into the national curriculum. The delivery of FUNdamentals in sports clubs should be through governing body sports coaches in sport-specific sessions (and be guided by their respective interpretation of the LTAD model). This delivery should manifest itself in an inclusive manner to account for the diversity in ability across able-bodied and disabled participants.

2 The National Curriculum

This section addresses the links between FUNdamentals and the national curriculum. Clearly, the school is the single environment in which virtually 100% of children have the opportunity to be exposed to sport and physical activity. The national curriculum provides a detailed guide on the provision and teaching of children in different subject areas in each of its Key Stages.

During Key Stage 1 (ages 5–7, school years 1–2), pupils should be taught the appropriate knowledge, skills and understanding through dance activities, games activities and gymnastic activities.

The following are taken from the National Curriculum online: http://curriculum.qcda.gov.uk

Dance activities

Pupils should be taught to:

- use movement imaginatively, responding to stimuli, including music, and performing basic skills (eg travelling, being still, making a shape, jumping, turning and gesturing)

- change the rhythm, speed, level and direction of their movements

- create and perform dances using simple movement patterns, including those from different times and cultures

- express and communicate ideas and feelings.

Games activities

Pupils should be taught to:

- travel with, send and receive a ball and other equipment in different ways

- develop these skills for simple net, striking/fielding and invasion-type games

- play simple, competitive net, striking/fielding and invasion-type games that they and others have made, using simple tactics for attacking and defending.

Gymnastic activities

Pupils should be taught to:

- perform basic skills in travelling, being still, finding space and using it safely, both on the floor and using apparatus

- develop the range of their skills and actions (eg balancing, taking off and landing, turning and rolling)

- choose and link skills and actions in short movement phrases

- create and perform short, linked sequences that show a clear beginning, middle and end and have contrasts in direction, level and speed.

Many of the skills and abilities that the national curriculum seeks to develop are similar to those identified in the FUNdamentals stage of LTAD. The terminology may be different, but the principles are the same. Table 2 illustrates the similarities between FUNdamentals and the requirements of the national curriculum. National curriculum PE, delivered well, will include almost all of the elements of a FUNdamentals programme.

Table 2: Similarities between FUNdamentals and national curriculum requirements

	Focus	Content	Curriculum Guidance
Foundation (3–5 years)	• FUNdamentals of Movement (FoM)	• Balance (static and simple dynamic) • Coordination (mainly internal) • Agility (simple movements)	Develop bodily control, large- and small-scale movements Improve coordination, control and ability to climb, balance, swing, slide, tumble, throw, catch and kick etc Respond to rhythm, adjust speed, change direction, negotiate space, jump and land Increase control over an object by touching, pushing, patting, throwing or catching it
	• Introduction and application of FoM within fundamental movement skills	• Run, jump, hop, gallop, skip, climb • Throw, catch, strike, bounce, trap, kick	
Key Stage 1 (5–7 years)	• Continued FoM	• Balance (dynamic) • Coordination (internal and external) • Agility (more complex movements)	Dance – basic skills (eg travelling, being still, jumping and turning); change rhythm, speed, level and direction of movement Games – travel, send and receive objects in different ways; develop skills for net, striking/fielding and invasion games Gym – basic skills (eg travelling, being still, finding space); develop range of skills (eg balancing, taking off and landing, turning and rolling)
	• Development of fundamental movement skills	• Run, jump, hop, gallop, skip, climb • Throw, catch, strike, bounce, trap, kick	
	• Introduction of general games skills	• Invasion • Net/wall • Striking/fielding	
Key Stage 2 (7–11 years)	• Development of general games skills • Introduction and development of sport-specific techniques and skills (eg tennis, cricket, netball)	• Invasion • Net/wall • Striking/fielding • Games for understanding • Major skill learning stage – all basic sports skills should be learnt • Mental/cognitive and emotional development	Dance – range of movement patterns, stimuli and accompaniment Games – play and create small-sided and modified net, striking/fielding and invasion games; use skills, tactics and apply basic principles of attack and defence Gym – create and perform fluent sequences on floor and apparatus; vary level, speed and direction within these Athletics – explore precision, speed, power, stamina and pacing oneself; use run, jump and throw skills singly and combined

3 Governing Bodies of Sport and Sports Clubs

Clubs and club coaches will play a vital role in the development of FUNdamentals. Children attending coaching in clubs for the first time will need to develop the physical skills that will help keep them in the club, playing the sport of their choice for a long time. In sports participation models, the child's first introduction to a sport is often at a local club. In order to develop sports skills, children need first to develop FUNdamental skills.

There may also be a stage where a child will decide to change sports. Quality FUNdamentals are transferable skills that will help him/her stay in any sport longer and be more successful.

Thirty-one governing bodies of sport have accepted and applied the principles of the LTAD model. FUNdamentals is at the base of their sport-specific participant development models and their associated athlete/player development programmes.

Tennis was one of the first governing bodies to adopt an LTAD model for the development of players, doing so in 2003 when the Lawn Tennis Association published their LTAD model for clubs, coaches and parents. At the base of the tennis model was the FUNdamentals stage, which at that time covered the years 5/6–9/10. The latest version of the tennis LTAD pathway is shown opposite, with the stages relevant to FUNdamentals highlighted below. Balance, especially, is an issue in tennis, which is a one-sided sport. It is needed by players to play shots at extreme range, for recovery and for moving quickly.

> As a youngster, I was brought up in a club that placed a strong emphasis on high-quality skill development. That skill base has allowed me to enjoy paddlesport over the years. Now my passion lies in exploring new places with friends and family.
>
> **Jeannette, sea kayaker**
>
> ***Preparing for a Life in Sport: A Guide to Good Practice for all People Involved in Paddlesport* leaflet**

8 – 10

Potential developing
- Wider involvement in tennis, but playing other sports
- Directed to specialised programme & coach
- Coaching input from track record performance coach
- Competitive involvement
- Every aspect of game developing
- Appropriate sports science
- Significant parental commitment starts

5 – 8

Learn fundamentals
- First experiences (fun, organised, competitive, purposeful)
- Regular physical activity including tennis
- Structured and flexible programme; increasing
- Family awareness of tennis opportunities
- Early Talent ID at club level

3 – 5

Early exposure & experience
- Tots sessions. Bats and balls
- Development of coordination

0 – 3

- Genetic make-up
- Environment

Figure 6: The Lawn Tennis Association's LTAD programme

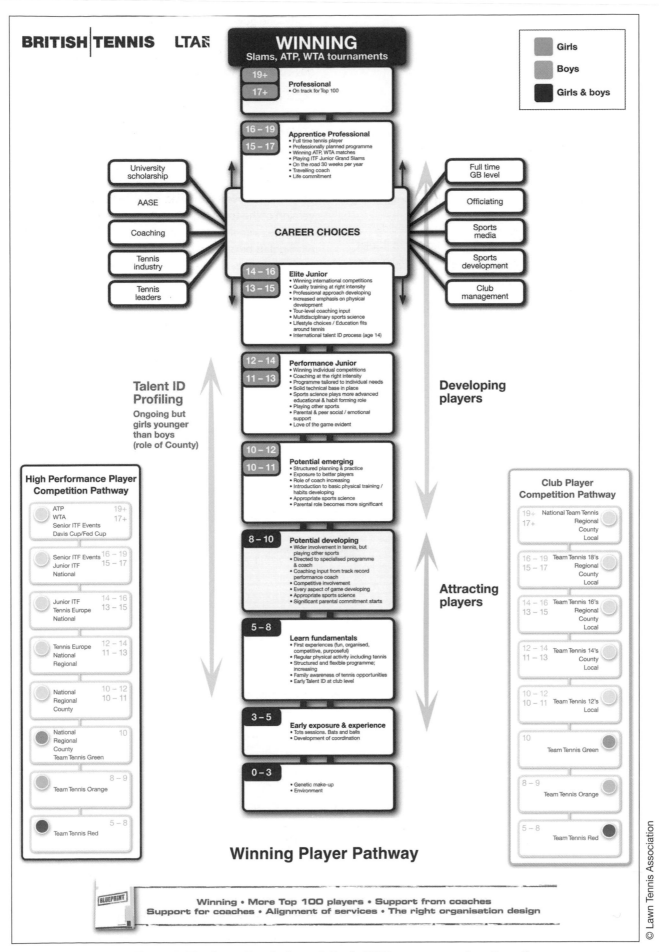

BRITISH TENNIS LTA

WINNING
Slams, ATP, WTA tournaments

Girls
Boys
Girls & boys

19+ / **17+** — **Professional**
• On track for Top 100

16 – 19 / **15 – 17** — **Apprentice Professional**
• Full time tennis player
• Professionally planned programme
• Winning ATP, WTA matches
• Playing ITF Junior Grand Slams
• On the road 30 weeks per year
• Travelling coach
• Life commitment

University scholarship
AASE
Coaching
Tennis industry
Tennis leaders

CAREER CHOICES

Full time GB level
Officiating
Sports media
Sports development
Club management

14 – 16 / **13 – 15** — **Elite Junior**
• Winning international competitions
• Quality training at right intensity
• Professional approach developing
• Increased emphasis on physical development
• Tour-level coaching input
• Multidisciplinary sports science
• Lifestyle choices / Education fits around tennis
• International talent ID process (age 14)

12 – 14 / **11 – 13** — **Performance Junior**
• Winning individual competitions
• Coaching at the right intensity
• Programme tailored to individual needs
• Solid technical base in place
• Sports science plays more advanced educational & habit forming role
• Playing other sports
• Parental & peer social / emotional support
• Love of the game evident

Talent ID Profiling

Ongoing but girls younger than boys (role of County)

Developing players

10 – 12 / **10 – 11** — **Potential emerging**
• Structured planning & practice
• Exposure to better players
• Role of coach increasing
• Introduction to basic physical training / habits developing
• Appropriate sports science
• Parental role becomes more significant

High Performance Player Competition Pathway

ATP	19+
WTA	17+
Senior ITF Events	
Davis Cup/Fed Cup	
Senior ITF Events	16 – 19
Junior ITF	15 – 17
National	
Junior ITF	14 – 16
Tennis Europe	13 – 15
National	
Tennis Europe	12 – 14
National	11 – 13
Regional	
National	10 – 12
Regional	10 – 11
County	
National	10
Regional	
County	
Team Tennis Green	
Team Tennis Orange	8 – 9
Team Tennis Red	5 – 8

8 – 10 — **Potential developing**
• Wider involvement in tennis, but playing other sports
• Directed to specialised programme & coach
• Coaching input from track record performance coach
• Competitive involvement
• Every aspect of game developing
• Appropriate sports science
• Significant parental commitment starts

Attracting players

5 – 8 — **Learn fundamentals**
• First experiences (fun, organised, competitive, purposeful)
• Regular physical activity including tennis
• Structured and flexible programme; increasing
• Family awareness of tennis opportunities
• Early Talent ID at club level

3 – 5 — **Early exposure & experience**
• Tots sessions. Bats and balls
• Development of coordination

0 – 3
• Genetic make-up
• Environment

Club Player Competition Pathway

National Team Tennis	19+
Regional	17+
County	
Local	
Team Tennis 18's	16 – 19
Regional	15 – 17
County	
Local	
Team Tennis 16's	14 – 16
Regional	13 – 15
County	
Local	
Team Tennis 14's	12 – 14
County	11 – 13
Local	
Team Tennis 12's	10 – 12
Local	10 – 11
Team Tennis Green	10
Team Tennis Orange	8 – 9
Team Tennis Red	5 – 8

Winning Player Pathway

BLUEPRINT
Winning • More Top 100 players • Support from coaches
Support for coaches • Alignment of services • The right organisation design

Figure 6: The Lawn Tennis Association's LTAD programme (continued)

Over time, a number of sports have introduced their own sport-specific LTAD models, based on the generic model. Those mentioned in this resource are listed in the Bibliography under Pankhurst (2005/2006/2007). Two of them are shown in Figures 7 and 8.

Rugby football league is a team sport in which players begin to specialise in the early and mid-teens, but the sport has an LTAD model that includes all stages. The FUNdamentals stage is shown below.

Swimming is an individual sport in which swimmers can specialise at an early age. Again, the sport has adapted all stages of the generic LTAD model to meet the needs of swimming as a sport.

The important factor in all three models shown is that FUNdamentals includes the basic physical skills that are vital components for development in all sports.

A more detailed summary of the way in which another governing body of sport – British Gymnastics – has adapted the generic LTAD model is given on the next page.

FUNdamentals
Chronological age
Girls: 6–8 years
Boys: 6–9 years

Important to develop:
FUNdamental Movement Skills.

Focus on developing:
• agility, balance and coordination
• running, jumping and throwing
• catching, kicking and striking
• body position and striking
• speed and power training
• other sports and games.

Volume/intensity of training:
• High volume
• Low intensity.

Number of rugby sessions per week:
• 2

Competition venues:
• Club/school.

Type of competition:
• Mini Rugby rallies and festivals.

Ratio of competition and training:
• No formal competition.

Coaches:
• Levels 1–2.

Figure 7: The Rugby Football League's LTAD model FUNdamentals stage

FUNdamentals
Chronological age
Males: 6–9 years
Females: 5–8 years

Important for:
Movement Literacy, FUN and Participation.

Focus on developing:
• general, overall development
• agility, balance and coordination
• running, jumping and throwing
• speed, power and endurance through FUN games – first speed window
• understanding of simple rules and sport ethics.

Swimming-specific skills:
• development of all four strokes.

Volume of training:
• skill acquisition.

Number and length of sessions per week:
• 5–6 sessions of general sport participation, to include land work and multi-sport activity
• 30–45-minute sessions.

Training hours per training week:
• sessional.

Periodisation programme:
• no periodisation
• high-quality, well-structured progressive programmes.

Type of competition:
• club championships
• intra-club competitions
• local/mini leagues.

Amount of competition:
• unlimited, informal and fun.

Coach qualifications:
• minimum level 2 and up to 4/5 – Level 1 can assist.

Figure 8: British Swimming's LTAD model

Gymnastics

Gymnastics is considered by some (Stafford, 2005) as an early-specialisation sport. Certainly, many parents recognise the sport as one that their children can start at a young age. British Gymnastics has responded to this demand with a structured training programme for coaches and a structured activity programme that children can start at pre-school age.

> *It would be a huge advantage for all young cricketers to have taken part in gymnastics activity at a young age, as this would give them the key movement and balance skills that underpin our sport.*
>
> **Pete Ackerley, Head of Development, England and Wales Cricket Board**
>
> *Preparing for a Life in Sport: A Guide to Good Practice for all People Involved in Gymnastics leaflet*

Many children do not continue into competitive gymnastics, but they take the benefits of a movement programme based on fun, fundamental movement skills and physical competence into other sports.

The children who become competitive gymnasts do so because they have an aptitude to learn skills – *physical literacy* – an ability to perform skills – *physical capacity* – and an appetite to enjoy the discipline and dedication of the sport. The level of skill and physical development shown by successful gymnasts proves what it is possible for young people to achieve.

The very young age at which children start gymnastics means that fun activities, based on children's natural desire to play and master skill challenges, are essential. The importance of the FUNdamentals of Movement ABCs is also clear. However, the sport has its own interpretations of these terms, just as other sports do. Agility in gymnastics is shown in many individual moves, such as rolls and cartwheels; balance is demonstrated in one-leg stands, handstands and headstands, and coordination is shown when agility and balance are linked together, as well as in developing dance and choreography skills.

Although the exact gymnastics interpretation of the ABCs is not necessarily the same as the general sport interpretation, the similarities are obvious. However, the physical development work done in gymnastics to ensure the acquisition of physical literacy is different to other sports. Gymnastics coaches consider body preparation and physical conditioning to be important because these give children the physical capacity to learn and master the skills required in gymnastics. This development work is initially fun-based with young children, although it ultimately becomes a personalised, specific training programme, developing the strength and flexibility needed in the sport.

Balance invariably requires strength, coordination frequently involves mobility to place limbs in the required position, and agility can be optimised with power and speed. An early learning gymnastics programme links physical literacy (ABC) with physical capacity (strength, suppleness, stamina and speed) in a fundamental way that will enhance both the gymnastics skills and the sports skills that children need in their ongoing physical development.

4 FUNdamentals Inclusion

The FUNdamentals of Movement programme is completely inclusive and can also be developed appropriately for all young disabled people.

Focusing and developing the fundamental abilities of all young people will ensure they have the skills to engage in participation opportunities and also have a strong foundation skill base to build sport-specific skills. It is important that the abilities of all young people are recognised and developed from participation to performance. It is essential coaches identify abilities and set challenging individual goals in an environment that is fun, engaging and appropriate.

The key FUNdamental skills can be developed in any coaching session with the application of high-quality coaching principles.

Try using the STEP principle to develop all your coaching sessions and make them participant-centred:

S – Space (change the space in which the activity is taking place in order to achieve personal goals)

T – Task (change the type of activity in order to achieve personal goals)

E – Equipment (change the type and size of equipment being used in order to achieve personal goals)

P – People (change the people who are involved in order to achieve personal goals).

Adapted from Stevenson, 2007

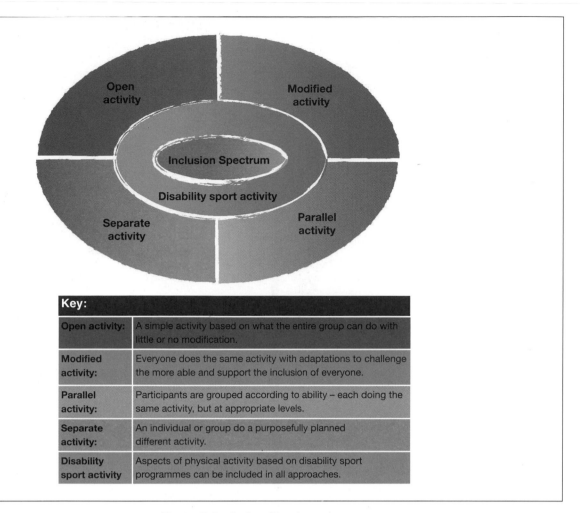

Key:	
Open activity:	A simple activity based on what the entire group can do with little or no modification.
Modified activity:	Everyone does the same activity with adaptations to challenge the more able and support the inclusion of everyone.
Parallel activity:	Participants are grouped according to ability – each doing the same activity, but at appropriate levels.
Separate activity:	An individual or group do a purposefully planned different activity.
Disability sport activity	Aspects of physical activity based on disability sport programmes can be included in all approaches.

Figure 9: Inclusion Spectrum
© Stevenson and Black
(adapted from Stevenson, 2007)

Sport has been an integral part of my life for as long as I can remember. My parents always encouraged me to try a variety of sports. I think it is important to give children such opportunities, even though I am a professional badminton player, I still enjoy playing other sports when time (and coaches) permit.

Gail Emms
International player and Olympic silver medallist

Preparing for a Life in Sport: A Guide to Good Practice for all People Involved in Badminton leaflet

The Inclusion Spectrum shown in Figure 9 could also be used to develop FUNdamentals with young disabled participants/performers. The different methods of coaching groups of different abilities can be very useful.

Parallel activity: Participants grouped according to ability – each doing the same activity, but at the appropriate levels.

5 FUNdamentals and Parents

Both Active Start and FUNdamentals are important stages towards lifelong enjoyment of health and sport. The key components of balance, coordination and agility need to be learnt during these stages. These stages are also the time when children start to interact with others, develop interests and hobbies, and learn the concept of right and wrong. Sport itself requires teamwork, fair play, sportsmanship, respect, rules and problem-solving skills that transfer into life skills. In some senses, therefore, sport is a preparation for life.

The FUNdamentals stage is the time when many children are introduced to specific sports for the first time. Children take up different sports for many and varied reasons – coaches coming into school, friends attending classes and clubs, parents' interests, and television. Sport has become big business and parents and children are reminded daily of the glamour of high wages and the lifestyles of sports stars. Parents also forget that children playing sport is not the same as adults playing sport. Young children do not have the same experience base or abilities as adults. They do not understand the processes or outcomes of becoming a high-quality athlete. Unfortunately, there are increasing instances of parents becoming overly involved in their children's sport. Examples of extreme and poor behaviour at junior sporting events, ranging from unnecessary and inappropriate involvement to abuse of referees and officials, encouraging their children to cheat or being evicted from matches and competitions, are becoming common.

The 'parent problem' has become more and more serious for many sports. As a result, many governing bodies of sport, and the sports industry in general, are spending time, money and effort trying to educate parents about how to support and nurture children in sport. Football has launched a programme called Soccer Parent, which aims to raise the standards of parental behaviour and knowledge; the International Tennis Foundation has a comprehensive document entitled *Being a Better Tennis Parent* and the Lawn Tennis Association has a Parents area on its website that

considers everything from behavioural problems to maximising potential.

The BBC Sport Academy website suggests some common problems associated with parents:

- *Putting children under so much pressure that they do more damage to their kids than good.*

- *Thinking that, because they pay expensive club or coaching fees, their children should, or can, win every single game.*

- *Fulfilling their own sporting dreams through their children without thinking about the children.*

- *Forgetting or ignoring the fact that kids may just want to have fun and may be happy to excel at a lower competitive level. Often, children just want to play with their friends.*

- *Parental behaviour and ambitions that make kids feel pressured and may cause them embarrassment in front of their friends.*

- *Pushing kids into being a professional athlete when all they want to do is play a sport.*

- *Forgetting that only a small percentage of kids who start a sport will make a living out of it and many do not even continue with that sport.*

- *Understanding that the child's enjoyment, growth and development should be the main priority.*

www.bbc.co.uk/sportacademy/parent
(no longer available)

The advice on the British Tennis Parents website for parents is:

Always remember that it is where your child ends up that is the most important thing. Every parent knows this and believes fully in this, but it is easy to lose sight of that fact.

There are many skills and personal qualities that parents want their children to develop as they grow up but, for now, remember to focus on the following long-term objectives, to:

- *carry on playing their whole life*

- *enjoy the challenge of competition*

- *learn the discipline of working hard and improving over the long term*

- *maximise their potential.*

www.britishtennisparents.com
(no longer available)

© Jason O'Brien/Action Images Limited

The FUNdamentals stage is one of the initial stages of the LTAD model that will hopefully lead children down one of two pathways – either lifelong participation in sport for enjoyment, health and happiness or, for a small minority, the experience of the elite side of sport. Parents need to understand the process and long-term nature of athlete/player development and the importance of the LTAD model so their children can achieve their potential and goals in sport.

It is obvious that, at the FUNdamentals stage of a child's development, the parent can be both a major positive and negative influence. It is at this stage that a child's sporting career and direction could be determined. FUNdamentals of Movement underpins all sports and all the skills required to develop sporting prowess. The FUNdamentals stage is also the ideal opportunity for parents to have fun playing with their children, helping in their development, being supportive in terms of finance and transport and, more importantly, setting good behavioural standards. Parents who spend 5–10 minutes every day with their children, testing each other's stork balance, playing Buckaroo, developing throwing and catching (with both hands) and having a good time are creating a good base for their children. All athletes need to be inspired throughout their career and children can get that inspiration from parents who spend quality time playing and developing key skills.

> *Of course, inspiration is not everything. Youngsters have to be physically educated in the correct manner. I am an unrelenting believer that the two key activities for youngsters under 10 should be swimming…and also basic gymnastics.*
>
> **Goodbody, 2007**

However, the parent's role should go beyond playing with their children, providing transport and providing inspiration. Parents also shape a child's psychological development. Research has shown that parents can influence a child's motivation, perceived competence and enjoyment in sport. Parental feedback and behaviour can affect how long a child stays involved in sport, as well as influencing a child's perception of his/her progress. Furthermore, the emphasis that a parent places on winning (the outcome), versus improving a skill, reinforces and determines what a child considers to be success in sport. In addition, how a parent behaves before, during and after a competition can cause great anxiety in the child and consequently affect performance, development and enjoyment.

Finally, many parents feel it is important to have a balance between sporting and educational development. Parents can sometimes feel pressured to ensure that sport is not taking place at the expense of education. Some parents can feel powerless and intimidated by teachers and coaches, who both make demands on their children's time.

A number of websites and articles give advice and support to parents in terms of how they should behave.

Top tips from *Sport Rage – A prevention guide for parents* suggest the following:

- *Emphasise trying hard and having fun, not winning.*

- *Don't pressure your child; it's their game, not yours.*

- *Never criticise or ridicule your child's performance.*

- *Discuss what your child enjoyed about the game.*

- *Be a good role model.*

- *Cheer and acknowledge good play from both teams and players.*

- *Be enthusiastic, but don't yell instruction.*

- *Always set a positive example.*

In sports coach UK's quarterly magazine, *Coaching Edge,* Issue 9, Melina Timson-Katchis also gives guidelines on parental behaviour:

What should parents do?

- *Listen to their children and accept their abilities.*

- *Support their children in sport and school, irrespective of their success and failure.*

- *Help children understand that the emphasis of participating is not on winning but on giving their best, having fun and learning.*

- *Help children understand the importance and benefits of a good education in addition to developing their extra-curricular interests.*

- *Get involved – volunteer their time, practise with their child, attend games and show they care.*

- *Provide children with proper equipment and clothing.*

- *Stay up to date with how a child is doing, both in sport and school.*

- *Listen to the coach.*

- *Get to know the teachers.*

- *Encourage children to take responsibilities for their actions.*

- *Encourage children to develop further interests in other sports, as well as out of sport.*

- *Allow children to set their own goals.*

- *Keep the teacher or coach informed if the child is ill or injured.*

- *Make sure that the child is eating and sleeping properly.*

- *Be a good role model.*

Adapted from Timson-Katchis, 2007

Finally, the BBC Sport Academy suggests:

If you are concerned over your involvement and influence as a parent, these 10 questions may help:

1   *Is my child having fun?*

2   *Am I being too competitive about my child winning?*

3   *Do I have realistic expectations of my child?*

4   *How should I behave if I disagree with a referee's decision?*

5   *Do I need to keep check on my behaviour?*

6   *How is my child feeling at the end of the game?*

7   *How do I behave when my child loses?*

8   *Do I get carried away when my child performs well?*

9   *Is sport taking priority over other activities in my child's life?*

10   *Am I putting too high expectations on myself?*

www.bbc.co.uk/sportacademy/parent
(no longer available)

In summary, a parent's role in the child's development in sport is vital in a number of different ways. In terms of developing FUNdamentals of Movement, the role is similar to the coach's. In some cases, it can be more important; for example, in helping the child to develop confidence, as well as the skill set to stay engaged in sport.

Summary

Section One of this resource examined the principles of LTAD and the importance of FUNdamentals in giving young children a high-quality base of movement skills. It has reviewed coaching practice and considered the differences in approach that are necessary to help young children on the road to a lifelong involvement in sport and physical activity.

Section Two will concentrate on the practical application of the principles and information from Section One. It includes detailed analyses of balance, coordination and agility and gives coaches ideas for games and activities that can be used with young children.

Section Two

The Practical Application of the FUNdamentals of Movement

FUNdamentals

> *When I was young, I had great fun with my friends doing lots of different sports. I didn't realise that all the different movements involved would give me a strong basis upon which to build when I began, at the age of 15, to specialise in netball. I not only understood how to be more effective in the international game, but also when and where to apply these skills.*
>
> **Amanda Newton,**
> **Former England Captain**
>
> ***Preparing for a Life in Sport: A Guide to Good Practice for all People Involved in Netball* leaflet**

Throughout Section One, the language of FUNdamentals used a number of different terms:

- FUNdamentals – meaning both FUNdamentals of Movement and fundamental movement skills

- multi-skill

- physical literacy.

While all of these terms are very closely linked, have similar meanings and overlap in their use, an understanding of their place in the progression of skill development can be gained from Figure 10.

Figure 10 shows the progression of skills in the different terminologies. It is very important that coaches understand this progression. The blocks – or stages – in this diagram show the pathway or continuum for the development of basic to sport-specific skills.

As an example, *balance* is one of the FUNdamentals of Movement in the first block of the continuum (together with coordination and agility).

Balance then becomes a component of every fundamental movement skill (eg run, jump, hop, catch, kick, skip and throw) in the second block.

Within the Fundamental Sports Skills block, *jumping* (which depends on good balance) is a necessary skill in all groups of sport (ie invasion, net/wall, striking and fielding games).

Finally, in the Sport-specific Skills block at the top of the continuum, *jumping* is an important skill used in netball.

Other generic skills can also be taught as part of the FUNdamentals continuum:

- fun

- social behaviour

- ethics

- teamwork

- strategy/tactics

- problem solving

- trajectories

- speed of movement or objects.

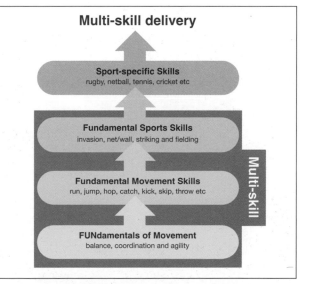

Figure 10: FUNdamentals continuum

The FUNdamentals of Movement – Agility, Balance and Coordination

The FUNdamentals are the ABCs – agility, balance and coordination. A child is considered to have **physical literacy** when all three of these skills are at a reasonable level for the child's age. Coaches need to consider the order in which they would coach each component of FUNdamentals, asking whether there is an order in which the skills should be taught and whether an order different to A, B, C would help children make progress. Possible orders could be:

A–B–C; A–C–B; B–C–A; C–A–B; C–B–A; or B–A–C.

In order to answer these questions, it is necessary to understand the terms themselves. In Section One (pages 22–25), it was noted that many governing bodies of sport have different interpretations of balance; for example, balance for tennis is not the same as for gymnastics. However, in terms of the first stage of the continuum, the generic definition is important. The definition for each element of FUNdamentals is given below, so coaches can decide the order in which they should be taught.

Balance

Balance is defined as a state in which a body or object remains reasonably steady and stable. Balance (equilibrium) is established when the centre of gravity (CoG) is over the base of support. The body will then be stable.

Coordination

Coordination is defined as the skilful and balanced sequencing of the body and its segments to produce movement of the body and generate force.

Agility

Agility is defined as the ability of the body to change direction and stop and start quickly and accurately while maintaining balance. Agility is the movement of the body at speed when it is both balanced and coordinated. To be agile, the body must move quickly and skilfully in different directions. It must also start and stop while maintaining stability.

The word that is repeated in all three definitions is **balance**. Coordination requires balance and agility needs both balance and coordination.

Thus, the FUNdamentals of Movement should be taught in the order of balance, coordination and agility.

The Principles of the FUNdamentals of Movement

Each aspect of FUNdamentals has underlying principles that, when understood and applied, can develop that FUNdamental in a logical manner. The workshop 'Introduction to the FUNdamentals of Movement' explores the lower-order principles of each of the ABCs, which are listed on the following pages. Coaches should consider these principles first when they are working with young children.

© Richard Heathcote/Action Images Limited

Principles of balance, coordination and agility are developed in more detail in sports coach UK's FUNdamentals of Movement workshop series. The new, advanced workshops review these lower-order principles and then examine more complex high-order principles. These principles should be considered once the lower-order principles are in place.

This section will thus provide some bridging information between the introductory course and the advanced workshop.

Principles of Balance

The lower-order principles are as follows:

1 Height of CoG

The lower the CoG, the greater the stability of the body.

2 Centre and base

Balance is achieved when the CoG is over the supporting base.

3 Losing balance

The further the CoG is from the centre of the supporting base, the less stable the body becomes. A larger base of support allows the CoG to move further in a given direction without losing stability.

The higher-order principles are as follows:

4 Extending the base

A larger base of support allows the CoG to move further in a given direction without losing stability.

5 Positioning the CoG

The initial position of the CoG, in relation to the base of support, can be used to advantage in moving quickly and maintaining stability when the body has forces acting against it.

6 Counterbalance (equal and opposite force)

When a body segment moves away from the centre, the CoG shifts in that direction. If the CoG moves outside the base of support, another segment of the body must move in the opposite direction to act as a counterbalance. External implements (eg sports equipment) and forces generated by the body can also displace the CoG.

7 Moving forces

When a moving force is applied to the body, the width of the base should be increased in the direction of the force to compensate for the shift in the CoG and to keep it within the base and maintain stability.

Principles of Coordination

The lower-order principles are as follows:

1 Organising limbs

The synchronisation of limbs to function together is closely linked to mental organisational abilities and should be considered along a continuum from simple (unilateral) to complex (contralateral). Crossing the body midline is a key coordination milestone.

2 Generating force

The speed of a ball, body or implement is determined by the speed of the last body segment at the time of contact or release. Therefore, the build-up of force or transfer of momentum along a chain from one body segment to the next is critical. Each body segment should be moved at the instant the previous segment begins to slow down, with larger, slower body segments moving first and smaller, lighter, faster segments moving later in the chain. This is called the kinematic chain.

3 Generating force

A longer lever arm and length of time over which force is applied leads to greater speed at the end point. Backswing, full extension of the limbs at release/contact and complete follow-through facilitates this increase in speed, as do artificial additions to the limb (eg racket, bat, club, stick).

The higher-order principles are as follows:

4 Differentiating force

Projecting a body or object through space requires the development of sufficient force to overcome its mass and gravity. The flight path depends on the combined effect of the amount of force generated, the weight of the body/object and the angle/height of release.

5 Speed and accuracy

The time and precision the movement can be carried out in and with while initiating and maintaining balanced, efficient movement.

6 Interception

Gravity acts to ensure the flight path of a body or object is symmetrical. Identifying the peak is key to anticipating the point of impact or interception. The highest point occurs at half the distance, where initial velocity gradually reduces to zero.

Principles of Agility

The lower-order principles are as follows:

1 Starting

The ability to change the position of the body from a static position to a different position in space.

2 Stopping

The ability to bring a body to a resting (static), controlled position as quickly and efficiently as possible.

3 Changing direction

The ability to reposition the body from moving in one direction to another, in a balanced and controlled manner.

The higher-order principles are as follows:

4 Rotation

The movement of the whole body or a body segment around an axis.

5 Reaction

The speed at which the body can start, stop or change direction in a controlled and balanced manner in response to a stimulus.

6 Complex

The ability to perform sequential movements of different body segments at different speeds at the same time.

© Alan Edwards

Coaching the FUNdamentals of Movement

Coaching is about a process of guided improvement that enables participants to feel more confident and competent. When coaching the basic FUNdamental skills of balance, coordination and agility, coaches need a structured process for observing the existing skill level of the child and deciding how to improve it.

FABB is an acronym that can be used as an observational tool to help the coaching of the FUNdamentals of Movement. Focusing on specific body segments can help the coach decide the skill level of the child.

F	–	Feet
A	–	Arms
B	–	Body
B	–	Brain (Head)

Balance

Balance can be either static or dynamic. This means the body can be stationary (in which case the balance is static) or moving (in which case the balance is dynamic and changing). Balance underpins all forms of human movement and all aspects of sporting movement. Many examples can be given in different sports (see Sport-specific Skills in the FUNdamentals continuum on page 31). These include Roger Federer's movement across the baseline to make a forehand drive down the line before moving back to a good position. The movement demonstrates highly skilled dynamic balance. Tiger Wood's golf swing highlights supreme power harnessed to supreme balance. Beth Tweddle's gymnastic skills combine strength, control and precision with balance.

All these performers also need coordination and agility in varying degrees, but they ultimately depend upon balance to control their movement. Controlled movement does not waste energy because it is efficient and effective and so reduces physical effort. It is precise, accurate and enables the optimum application of force to create maximum power. Controlled movement keeps the body in balance.

Balance and counterbalance depend on strength and flexibility to keep the body segments in a stable position when creating or reacting to a force. It is both possible and essential for the coach to develop strength and flexibility by challenging a child's balance in a variety of drills, activities and games.

If the child does not develop good static and dynamic balance then coordination and agility skill levels will be reduced.

Coaching Static and Dynamic Balance

Static balance can be developed at the early stages of coaching FUNdamentals. However, coaches will know the vital importance of coaching being fun and progressive. The ideas below could be used to develop static balance:

- maintaining ready positions for different sports

- practising keeping balance with a base of support of different sizes and shapes

- trying body positions of different animals

- changing the height of the body – balance on a base or cushion beam

- changing the stimulus – with eyes closed, with a partner, move or rotate arms and legs

- Simon Says

- press-up balance (make sure the children are on their knees)

- Buckaroo

- change levels from low to high to challenge balance

- musical balance

- statues

- happy bases/stances.

Inclusion – Balance
Applying STEP Principles

Stork Balance

- A person may position him/herself against a wall or other person to practise the stork balance position.

- Kneeling stork with more points of contact.

- A beanbag may be balanced on a body part for additional challenge.

- Support may be given to someone on a wobble board to experience the additional challenge.

Adapted from Stevenson, 2007

Many of these ideas can be linked to numeracy and literacy.

The **technical coaching points** of static balance are important to help children improve:

- **Feet** width of the base of support

- **Arms** arms (or legs) of support in counterbalance

- **Body** good posture so that the CoG is in the right position

- **Brain** head up, eyes forward.

Dynamic balance must also be developed at the early stages of coaching FUNdamentals. Being balanced while moving is an important skill. Dynamic balance can be fun to coach, but also needs to be progressive and increasingly challenge the child. The ideas below could be used to develop dynamic balance:

- Pacman with a variety of movements (see page 42)

- different ways of moving – hopping, jumping, skipping

- crossing the river – moving between different cones set at different distances

- animal movements – bear, camel (also link to gymnastic movements)

- obstacle courses

- hoop pulling

- different ways of walking – story walking, follow the leader

- moving sideways.

The **technical coaching points** of dynamic balance are important to help children improve:

- **Feet** flat on the floor, toes extended

- **Arms** may be held out away from the body to assist

- **Body** segments straight and still with knees slightly flexed.

- **Brain** head up, eyes forward, focused on a fixed point, watching and waiting to respond.

Coordination

At the FUNdamentals of Movement stage, children should develop coordinated movements in three main ways:

- unilaterally

- bilaterally

- contralaterally.

The majority of movement can be broken down, but also developed into these three types. Different children will have different skill levels in each type.

Unilateral movement is a movement of one side of the body. This could be standing still while waving with one hand, giving a high five or sticking a leg out.

Bilateral movement is movement of both sides of the body. This could be moving both arms up in the air, the right arm and right leg out, or a two-footed jump.

Contralateral movement is movement of opposite sides of the body. This is slightly more advanced. It could be either right leg and left arm or taking the right arm across the midline of the body to the left side.

Domes and Dishes (page 41) is a practical game for coaches to use to decide the different skill levels of a group of children. The following questions can help when observing children play the game:

- How do the children pick up the cones?
    - Unilaterally?
    - Bilaterally?
    - Contralaterally?

In reality, children will vary in the way they pick up the cones. The first few times they play, it will be unilaterally, focusing on one cone at a time. This gives the coach an excellent opportunity to consider the following:

- What is the most efficient movement?

- Do the children have a strategy and work out where the next cone is?

- What coaching points could be included?

Efficiency

The most efficient movement will be based upon the individual, but also on the next movement.

- The child could pick up a cone and then move to the right. For this, the most efficient movement is bilateral with the left leg and left hand because this enables a better and faster movement to the right.

- The child could pick up a cone and move forward to the next cone. For this, a contralateral movement is more efficient. To help the movement forward, the child will use the opposite arm and opposite leg.

Strategy

At the early stage of developing coordination, children tend to focus on one cone at a time. This gives the coach the opportunity to introduce tactics and movement efficiency. When the coach observes that a child moves poorly to the left either because of coordination or even balance, then this game could be used to work on these skills. The game can also be used to improve tactics and strategies by asking the children to pick up cones in a specific colour order (eg pick up a blue cone after a red cone).

Coaching Points

Important coaching points for Domes and Dishes would include those for:

- dynamic balance (page 36)

- unilateral, bilateral or contralateral coordination (pages 36–37).

There is also an opportunity for the coach to develop a variety of other skills at the same time, such as:

- spatial awareness

- distal/proximal movement

- teamwork

- communication

- problem solving

- tactics

- ethics

- numeracy and literacy.

Coordination is important for, and included in, throwing, catching, striking and fielding activities – all of these are fundamental movement skills (page 31).

Timing is a very important component of coordination. It is part of both the tempo and the rhythm of movement. **Tempo is the pace of the movement (ie how fast or slow the movement is). Rhythm is concerned with the differences and alternation of the pace of movement at different times.**

> *Rhythm is the underlying organisational pattern that gives order to music and dance.*
>
> **Fowler, 1994**

Movement that is skilful, well balanced and precisely timed is coordinated. When coaching FUNdamentals, coaches will find it relatively easy to observe children who have poor coordination because their movements seem clumsy, non-sequential, and lacking timing or rhythm. A simple exercise to observe rhythm and timing is to ask the children to clap to a rhythm set by the coach. Those children who struggle with coordination will either clap out of time or find it difficult to keep to the rhythm. To develop these skills with movement, coaches could try alternating three claps and three physical moves to help the children maintain a rhythm.

For example, studies of timing control under external pacing conditions in 6–11-year-old children with coordination problems highlight poor timing consistency when they are required to maintain a predetermined pace or to synchronise their tapping with an auditory metronome. (Geuze and Kalverboer 1987, 1993, 1994; Greene and Williams, 1993; Williams et al,1992).

Savelsbergh et al, 2003

Shadowing and mirroring are other excellent activities that can help children develop their coordination in a rhythmical and timed manner. They also give children the opportunity to explore and design their own patterns of movement and rhythm.

The **technical coaching points** of coordination are important to help children improve:

- **Feet**   in a well-balanced ready position

- **Arms**   extended or bent

- **Body**   balanced while moving, with eyes focused on target

- **Brain**   concentrating, watching and waiting to respond.

Inclusion – Coordination
Applying STEP Principles

Racket Skills

- Young person uses a table surface striking against a wall to practise a racket skill.

- Vary moving and stationary tasks.

- Explore strapping and lightweight bats, balloons and quoits.

- Introduce a feeder.

Adapted from Stevenson, 2007

Agility

Agility is the ability to control the body in dynamic situations. It involves moving quickly and skilfully, starting, stopping and then starting again, possibly in a different direction, while maintaining stability (dynamic balance).

Agility therefore requires children to have the first-level principles of balance (static and dynamic) and coordination and then include speed. Coaches need to be sure that balance and coordination skills are well developed before introducing speed of movement and body control.

The concepts of ground reaction force, momentum, rhythm, rotation and spin are all part of agility since the body is moving at speed in different directions. Coaches need to include these in different games and activities to help children develop agility.

The games should include:

- change of pace – this can involve ground reaction force

- use of many different patterns of movement

- change of direction – involving momentum, rhythm and rotation

- twisting and turning – using momentum, rhythm, rotation and spin.

Some fun games that develop agility are:

- dodgeball

- drop-catch ball

- invasion-type games

- obstacle courses

- slalom relays.

When the basic skills are in place, children then need to progress to the more complex fundamental movement skills (see pages 33–34) that involve different timings and combinations of movement – skipping, galloping, dribbling, running and catching, jumping, throwing etc.

The development of agility should also include controlled movements at speed from varying body positions:

- low to high

- fast to stop

- stop to fast

- side to side

- forward to back.

The **technical coaching points** of agility are important to help children improve:

- **Feet** in a well-balanced and appropriate position for the movement

- **Arms** close to the body, extended or bent

- **Body** dynamically balanced while moving at speed and under control to start, stop and change direction

- **Brain** concentrating and focused.

Examples of Different Games to Develop Balance, Coordination and Agility

Games

The games that follow are intended to help coaches develop the FUNdamentals of Movement skills in young children.

Each game has:

- considerations for the coach developing balance, coordination and agility

- observation points for the coach

- possible coaching points to enable the coach to develop the skills.

© Brandon Malone/Action Images Limited

Inclusion – Agility
Applying STEP Principles

Reacting to an Unseen Feed

- Increase or decrease the distance from the feed.
- Encourage a touch or a point to the direction the ball is coming from.
- Use a sound ball, slow-moving ball or give a net or glove to the catcher.
- Encourage the feeder to count down and give additional auditory and visual cues.

Adapted from Stevenson, 2007

Domes and Dishes
Observe and Analyse A, B and C

Considerations for the Coach

Balance

- The child's ability to slow down, bend down, pick up and turn over a cone without losing balance
- The child's ability to push off after picking up the cone without losing balance
- How the child uses the other arm, the non-standing leg and any counterbalance issues
- The base of support used by different children when turning the cone: one foot, two feet, wide base

Coordination

- Whether the child turns the cones contralaterally, reaching across the standing foot
- Whether the child turns a cone using one hand or both and the effect this has on balance

Agility

- The child's dodging abilities and if changes of direction are made off either foot
- Discernable changes of pace, made easier by changes in footwork patterns and body shape
- The time element that is used at different levels of ability.

Observation Points for the Coach

- Form and posture as the child bends down
- The position of the head and the visual focus
- Loss of balance and in which direction
- The use of the hands and the way the child turns the cone
- The ability of the child to turn and move in all directions
- The strategy different children use in deciding which cone to turn over next
- The understanding of different ways to pick up the cone
- The efficiency of movement towards the next cone.

Possible Coaching Points

- Explore counterbalance with arms and legs
- Static balance practice, crouching on one leg (use both sides)
- Footwork exercise to encourage quick feet
- Specific exercises to encourage left-handed and right-handed development
- Varying footwork to pick the cones up in order to improve efficient movement to the next cone
- Perceptual vision activities.

Pacman

Observe and Analyse A, B and C

Considerations for the Coach

Balance

- The child's ability to maintain static and dynamic balance through a range of movements and activities

- The child's ability to change direction while maintaining dynamic balance

- The posture and control of the CoG

Coordination

- The child's ability to coordinate alternate foot/arm movements effectively when travelling

- The child's ability to change between one-foot and two-feet patterns

- Changes in methods of moving

- The coordinated use of the arms and movement

Agility

- Increases and decreases in travelling speed

- The child's ability to change direction at varying speeds while maintaining both balance and coordination.

Observation Points for the Coach

- How the child balances when moving in a variety of directions and travelling methods

- The position of the CoG as the child moves

- The posture and head position

- The difference in right- and left-side movement when travelling.

Possible Coaching Points

- Changes of travelling patterns between walking/jogging/running/skipping/ sidestepping/striding etc

- Additional activities when travelling – passing equipment, high fives etc

- Add variation of movement patterns with cones, hurdles etc

- Change in direction – travelling forward, backward and sideways (both right and left leg leading).

Buckaroo

Observe and Analyse A, B and C

Considerations for the Coach

Balance

- The child should be able to challenge and change the position of the CoG in relation to static balance positions

- The child should be able to control movement and balance in a variety of positions and through different CoG positions

- Whether the child can find different points of balance

Coordination

- The child's ability to manage different muscle groups and limbs to counterbalance challenges to the CoG

Agility

- The child's body control, and the speed at which the child changes direction

- The child's body posture and balance when stopping, starting and changing direction.

Observation Points for the Coach

- The child's ability to challenge his/her own balance abilities

- The position of the head to maintain balance

- The starting position, the ability of the child to increase/decrease the base of support, challenge the CoG and use both strong and weaker body segments.

Possible Coaching Points

- Variation of starting positions from beginner to advanced bases of support

- The child chooses his/her own starting position

- Change to level of activity by using beams, wobble cushions etc

- Use strong and weak sides of the body.

Classic Hopscotch

Observe and Analyse A, B and C

Considerations for the Coach

Balance

- A child's ability to complete a section of the hopscotch grid without losing balance

- The control of balance through hopping, jumping and landing, both from and to one or two feet

Coordination

- The effective coordination of one-foot and two-feet patterns

- The use and movements of the arms, coordinated with the movement of the body

Agility

- The strength of a child in any particular movement

- The posture and position of the upper body

- The speed of movement from one section of the hopscotch grid to another.

Observation Points for the Coach

- The timing and rhythm in different movements

- The ability to balance as the child progresses forward

- The position of the CoG

- The difference, if any, between the left leg and right leg landing and hopping.

Possible Coaching Points

- Ask the children to stop briefly between each step to regain balance (or use a clap to stop them randomly)

- Suggest other footwork patterns to develop range of movement patterns

- Stabilise one-foot and two-feet landing and jumping.

Planning a FUNdamentals of Movement Programme

There are a variety of ways in which coaches can implement the FUNdamentals of Movement into a coaching programme for children aged 6–9. Planning is essential to ensure that the FUNdamentals are learnt in an effective progression and that the children develop the skills of balance, coordination and agility.

Figure 11 shows a simple 10-week FUNdamentals of Movement programme.

Week	Programme
1	Introduction/fun games/relays
2	Balance assessment
3	Balance
4	Coordination assessment
5	Coordination
6	Agility assessment
7	Agility
8	Development on balance, coordination and agility
9	Repeat week 8
10	Final assessment

Figure 11: FUNdamentals of Movement programme

When developing the programme, the coach must be sure what is being coached and know how the FUNdamentals skills fit into the session.

Children will take time to develop and progress FUNdamentals into higher-level skills. As has been discussed many times in this resource, the FUNdamentals are crucial to the development of other skills in sport. A vital part of coaching FUNdamentals skills is knowing what and how to observe what each child is doing and being able to help them accordingly. The examples given earlier in this section should help coaches with this process.

More FUNdamentals games and activities follow so that coaches have many ideas to fit into their coaching programme.

Ideas for Games

Balance Activity Ideas

- Balance beanbags on different parts of the body while performing a static or dynamic balance
- Balance on a small patch, on three points etc
- Children close their eyes while performing a balance
- Pass a ball or beanbag while balancing on one leg
- Pass a ball or beanbag while performing a static or dynamic balance on a bench
- In pairs, while holding hands, try to pull the partner off balance
- In a small group, hold a hoop and try to pull the others off balance
- Stand in a hoop, try to lift the hoop over the head while balancing
- Walk forwards/sideways/backwards along a line or bench
- Walk forwards/ sideways/backwards along a line or bench and step over or through objects
- Walk on stilts, along lines and use different pathways
- Balance on a wobble board
- Balance on a wobble board holding/ passing/touching an object
- How far/long can each child jump?
- Jump two-footed around the hands of a clock

Ideas for Games

Balance Activity Ideas (continued)

- Jump two-footed a quarter-turn – four turns to the right, three turns to the left, two turns to the right, one turn to the left
- Balance Tag
- Musical Statues
- Dragon's Treasure
- Follow My Leader
- Simon Says
- Animal Walks.

Ideas for Games

Coordination Activity Ideas

- Reaction Board with hands or feet
- Touch the Ball
- Touch the Spot
- Hand-clapping games
- High Five/Low Five
- Pass the Ball and Clap, using different combinations and techniques
- Swing skipping rope at side of body, skipping, cross-over skipping
- Pass ball in a circle or across circle
- Different stepping patterns
- Move to Music
- Pick up/Put Down the Beanbags
- Jumping backwards and forwards over a line or stick
- Jump in and out of a hoop
- Jump over the rope
- Reach the Ball
- Touch the Floor
- Dance Mats
- Ball and Chain
- Crab Football
- Follow My Leader.

Ideas for Games

Agility Activity Ideas

- Zigzag running, with equipment
- Triangle run
- Start, Stop and Change Direction
- Relay Races
- Sprint and Jog
- Catch Me if You Can
- North, South, East or West
- Follow My Leader
- Collect the Beanbag
- Rats and Rabbits
- Ducks and Drakes
- Steal It
- Train Tag
- Sprint-start Relay
- Beanbag Scramble
- Traffic Lights.

Assessing and Recording the Progress of Children

Coaches will find it invaluable to know and monitor the skill level of the children in each of the FUNdamentals of Movement skills. To do so, they need to know which principles of each FUNdamental (see pages 32–34) have been taught. The record sheets that follow are intended to help coaches check off the principles.

Record Sheet: **Balance**
BALANCE is defined as a state in which a body or object remains reasonably steady and stable.

Creating the base of support (static and stable) (*record activities*)

Shifting the CoG (*record activities*)

Dynamic balance activities (dynamic and changing) (*record activities*)

Games ideas that develop balance (*record activities*)

Record Sheet: Coordination
Coordination is defined as the skilful and balanced sequencing of the body and its segments to produce movement.

Developing coordination and movement of arms and legs:

- **Unilateral** (*record activities*)

- **Bilateral (symmetrical, asymmetrical)** (*record activities*)

- **Contralateral** (*record activities*)

Using rhythm to coordinate movement of arms or legs (*record activities*)

Shadowing (coordination with an external stimulus – watching another person) (*record activities*)

Coordination of muscle groups to produce force:

- **Jumping** (*record activities*)

- **Throwing (focus on hip rotation and separate actions of the upper and lower body)** (*record activities*)

Games ideas that develop coordination (*record activities*)

Record Sheet: Agility

Agility is defined as the ability of the body to change direction and stop and start quickly and effectively while maintaining balance.

Activities for developing individual timing and rhythm patterns (coordination) (*record activities*)

Activities for changing rhythm patterns, speeding up, slowing down and changing direction (*record activities*)

Games ideas that develop agility (*record activities*)

Conclusion – Why Coaches Should Help Children Develop FUNdamentals

If there is to be a cultural shift in how performance athletes are developed and also to tackle the nation's health issues at the same time, then coaches will need to play a vital role in developing the participation pathway. The FUNdamentals stage of the LTAD model is vital to this process. Coaches therefore will need to look at their own practice and bring it into line with the concept and practice of starting young children with the skills they will need for sport for the rest of their lives.

Every sport and coach would prefer to have athletes, rather than no athletes, in their programmes. It is easier. Athletes who can perform basic skills, such as running and jumping, throwing and catching, become athletes at a higher level.

Coach Reflection Point

Review the sports in Figure 12. Which sports can people play if they have the simple skill of catching a ball?

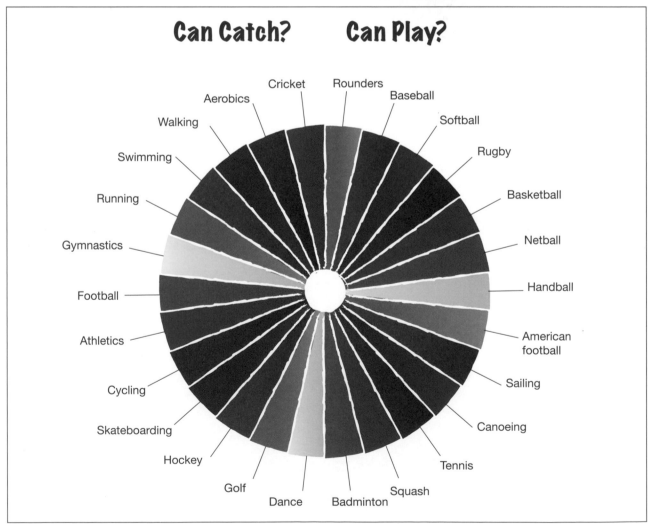

**Figure 12: Sports and the skill of catching a ball
(adapted from Jess, 2004)**

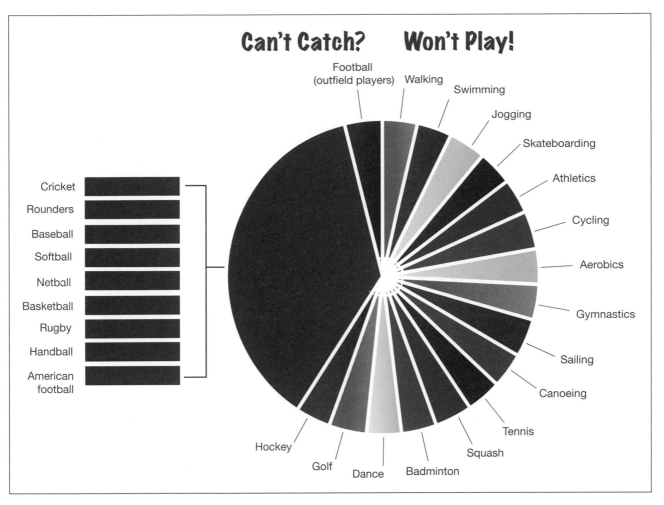

Figure 13: Sports in the red section involve the skill of catching a ball (adapted from Jess, 2004)

Summary

An analysis of Figure 13 shows the number of sports that require the simple skill of being able to catch a ball.

If the simple skill of catching is broken down into the components of the FUNdamentals, it is clear balance, coordination and agility are essential. Thus, if the FUNdamentals of Movement skills are not taught, then a person will not be able to learn the simple skill of catching a ball. The logical follow-up is that a person who cannot catch cannot play.

For most people, this will mean they will not play, and sport and physical activity cannot be part of their lifestyle.

This simple analogy underpins the content of this resource – for young people and adults to take part in sport and physical activity, they need to learn the FUNdamentals of Movement at an early age.

Glossary of Terms

A	Agility is defined as the ability of the body to change direction and stop and start quickly and accurately while maintaining balance.
Axis	An imaginary point around which a body or body parts may move/rotate.
B	Balance is defined as a state in which a body or object remains reasonably steady and stable.
Bilateral	Refers to the coordination of the same two limbs either side of a vertical axis.
C	Coordination is defined as the skilful and balanced sequencing of the body and its segments to produce movement.
Contralateral	Refers to the coordination of arms and legs on opposite sides of the vertical axis.
Differentiation	The process of applying learning that is appropriate to the stage of development of the learner, particularly in group learning environments.
FoM (FUNdamentals of Movement)	Principles that underpin both generic and sport-specific movement skills (ie ABCs).
Fundamental movement skills	Basic movement skills that include:

- walking
- running
- jumping
- throwing
- catching
- striking
- kicking
- skipping
- hopping.

Impulse	The product of force applied over time.
Inertia	The resistance of an object to change in motion, which is proportional to its mass.
Inter-limb coordination	The coordination of two limbs to function together.
Kinematic chain	A linkage of body parts involved in transferring forces/motion from one body segment to the next.
LTAD	Long-term athlete development.
Physical literacy	The acquisition of, and the ability to learn and use, a wide variety of basic physical skills, such as agility, balance, coordination, running, jumping and throwing.
Summation of forces	The progressive build-up of forces as limb segments are recruited to the kinematic chain.
Transfer of momentum	The transfer of the amount of motion possessed by a moving object.
YST	Youth Sport Trust.

Games Description Glossary

The following are simple descriptions to be used as guidelines. There are a variety of adaptations and ways for coaches to get the most out of their participants, such as allowing them to develop their own interpretations.

Balance

Balance Beanbags	Players walk around, moving in any direction, balancing a beanbag on their head or different parts of their body. Coaches can give them fun cues (eg 'touch the floor') to help develop their balance.
Balance on Patches	Players travel around and then, on a cue from the coach, balance on small patches of their body (eg hands, feet, elbows, knees). Coaches can use number initiatives to help them count and balance.
Balance Blind	The children try a variety of balance games included in static balance with their eyes closed. Coaches should remember to always make their practice safe.
Pass and Balance	In pairs or small groups, the children pass balls or other equipment while balancing a beanbag, cone or other piece of equipment on part of their body. Coaches can try varying the base of support from two legs to one leg etc and raising the players' height with a beam, cushion or bench for further progressions.
Push and Pull	In pairs, the children try to push and pull their partner off a spot or out of a hoop, challenging their balance. Coaches can try using different types of equipment (eg poles, hoops or bats) for more fun and challenge.

Hoop Balance	The children each stand in a hoop in a balanced position of their choice. They then try to raise the hoop over their head and back down again.
Balance Trails	The children try walking along a variety of challenging beams and benches of different heights and widths. Coaches should remember to always make their practice safe. Coaches can add some activities for the children to do while walking or moving and distractions for fun and development. Coaches should remember, when working with beams, benches and heights, to make sure they have taught their players to step off and control their balance for a safe dismount.
Stilts	The children can walk on stilts, small pots and larger pots to help develop their balance and movement in a fun manner.
Wobble Boards	The children can use wobble boards in the same way as stilts and beams. They can try working in pairs, and coaches can add games (eg Push and Pull, Pass the Ball) at a higher level of balance.
Clock Jumping	Coaches use the numbers on a clock to get players to jump and control their balance throughout the movement. Children start by jumping from 12 to one o'clock before developing to 12 to six o'clock etc. Participants can start with two feet then transfer to one when they are comfortable with their balance.
Balance Tag	Participants move around with one or two players 'on' (wearing bibs to identify them or even a cone on their head to develop their own balance). As the 'on' players tag others, those tagged have to hold a static balance position until someone frees them.
Musical Statues	As the music stops, all players must hold a static balance position of their choice.
Dragon's Treasure	The game is played in a small area (small because the emphasis is on balance) surrounding a hoop with a variety of equipment in it. Players have a set period of time to steal as much equipment as possible (one item at a time) and return it to a home base.
Follow My Leader	Playing in small groups or as one large group, the leader travels around a marked area while everyone else follows. As the coach says 'stop', the leader must hold a static balance position that all followers must duplicate.
Simon Says	A coach- or player-centred game in which all participants follow simple instructions. The coach or nominated participant calls out 'Simon says…' followed by a simple action and all players respond accordingly. If they move when the nominated participant calls out an action without 'Simon says…', they must continue to do another activity or static balance.
Animal Walks	The children explore travelling using the movements of a chosen animal. Players can choose their own animals and see how many different examples they can come up with. Coaches can add some music for fun. Participants can work in pairs or threes and exchange animal movements.

Coordination

Reaction Board	Players stand opposite each other. One makes a one-handed movement and his/her partner follows and touches his/her hand. They do 10 movements and then swap over. When they have developed a single movement on both hands, they can try using two hands as a progression.
Touch the Ball	Similar to Reaction Board, but one player moves a ball around (high or low, near or far) and his/her partner has to see how quickly he/she can touch the ball.
Touch the Spot	As above, but players can kneel or stand. They are surrounded by different coloured spots. When their partner calls out a colour, they must touch that colour spot with their hand or foot. Spots can be widened to allow players to step or jump to the appropriate colour.
High Five/Low Five	The children travel around a marked area. When the coach calls out 'high five' or 'low five', all players carry out the appropriate action with the person nearest to them. Participants can be allowed to make their own judgements and decisions.
Pass the Ball and Clap	Groups of players form a shape of their choice that is appropriate to the number in the group. As they pass the ball around the shape, they choose to clap once, twice or three times. It will be up to them to develop their own rhythmical pattern.
Skipping	After coaching basic skipping patterns, the coach allows players to develop different skipping techniques and patterns (including movement).

Pass the Ball	Groups of players form a shape of their choice that is appropriate to the number in the group. They then pass the ball in a variety of forms (eg bounce pass, chest pass, one-handed, two-handed).
Stepping	In groups, players develop travelling activities (eg hop-step-jump) and all players travel around a marked area in unison with the same movement patterns as each other.
Move to Music	Different types of music are played and participants move in different ways to the music. Fast and slow music and changes of tempo, rhythm and movement allow the children to explore different movements.
Pick Up/Put Down	This can be played as an activity, game or a competition. Players have a marked area to travel to where they pick up beanbags (or any other equipment) and return to base.
Stick Jumping	Players jump forwards, backwards or sideways over a stick or other equipment (eg a hoop or rope). This concentrates on control of balance, movement and landing. They can also explore other ways to jump over the stick.
Reach the Ball	As Touch the Ball, but this includes more distance or a change of height (eg with one player on a beam, wobble board or bench).
Touch the Floor	As above, with one player on a beam or moving along a beam with actions of touching the floor on both sides with different equipment, hands and patterns.
Dance Mats	Participants perform specific movement patterns to music. If no dance mats are available, use different coloured spots and actions associated with each colour.
Crab Football	This involves two teams with two sets of goals. Players crawl in a crab position, try to pass the ball, work together as a team, maintain and develop their balance and score in the opponents' goal.
Follow My Leader	As in Balance, with more direction appropriate to coordination.

Agility

Zigzag	At speed, players move in and out of cones and equipment set up around a marked area.
Triangle	The coach sets up a triangle of cones, with one, two or more players on each point of the triangle. The children develop acceleration and deceleration as they move to other points of the triangle. Players can try moving in different ways to the points of the triangle either laterally or vertically.
Start, Stop and Change Direction	With no boundaries in a safe, marked area, players develop agility through movement and spatial awareness by carrying out the appropriate movements (start, stop or change direction) as directed. Coaches can use coloured cones to enhance learning.
Relay Races	Coaches can try having different types of races that are not just linear.
Sprint and Jog	As in Start, Stop and Change Direction, in any suitable format, this helps players to understand different agility phases. Coaches can use a whistle or other form of stimulus to enhance participants' development.
Catch Me if You Can	As it suggests, one or two people try to catch as many people as they can in a set time.
North, South, East or West	Players travel around a marked area with four compass sections marked in the appropriate direction of the space. When the coach calls out one direction (eg north), all players head to the appropriate section as fast as they can.
Follow My Leader	As in Balance, with more direction appropriate to agility.
Collect the Beanbag	As above, but with more emphasis on agility.
Rats and Rabbits	Two lines of players face each other. One side is named rats and the other rabbits. The coach calls out 'rats' or 'rabbits'. The appropriate side turn and run to an end line and members of the other team try to tag them before they can reach the line. (This game is also known as Ducks and Drakes.)
Train Tag	This game starts off with one person chasing everyone else. As players are caught, they join the train to then try to catch the others. As more and more participants are caught, the train becomes bigger and more difficult to move.
Sprint-start Relay	This is run as a normal relay, with the emphasis on speed of movement.
Beanbag Scramble	A marked area is filled with beanbags. Players have a set time to collect as many beanbags as possible (one at a time) and return them to their designated area.
Traffic Lights	The coach holds up a coloured cone and the players, moving around a marked area, respond accordingly: red = stop; amber = jog travel; green = accelerate.

Bibliography

Baker, J., Côté, J. and Abernathy, B. (2003). Sport-specific practice and the development of expert decision-making in team ball sports. Journal of Applied Sport Psychology. 15, 12–25.

Balyi, I. (2001) 'Sport system building and long-term athlete development in British Columbia'. Canada: Sportsmed BC.

Côté, J., Baker, J. and Abernathy, B. (2003) 'From play to practice: A developmental framework for the acquisition of expertise in team sports', in Starkes, J. and Ericsson, K.A. (eds), *Expert Performance in Sports: Advances in Research on Sport Expertise*. Champaign, IL: Human Kinetics. ISBN: 978-0736041-52-2. pp. 89–113.

Dixon, S. (ed) (2004) 'Sport Rage – a prevention guide for parents', www.dsr.nsw.gov.au/publicat/detail.asp?pub=72

Fowler, C. (1994) *Music: Its Role and Importance in Our Lives*. New York: Glencoe. ISBN: 978-0-026555-65-4.

Geuze, R.H. and Kalverboer, A.F. (1987) 'Inconsistency and adaptation of timing of clumsy children', *Journal of Human Movement Studies*, 13, 421–32.

Geuze, R.H. and Kalverboer, A.F. (1993) 'Bimanual rhythmic coordination in clumsy and dyslexic children', in Valenti, S.S. and Pittenger, J.B. (eds) *Studies in Perception and Action II*. Hillsdale, NJ: Lawrence Erlbaum. ISBN: 978-0-805814-05-7. pp. 24–28.

Geuze, R.H. and Kalverboer, A.F. (1994) 'Tapping a rhythm: a problem for children who are clumsy and dyslexic', *Adapted Physical Activity Quarterly*, 11, 203–13.

Goodbody, J. (2007) 'Dedication's what you need', *coaching edge*, 9: 5.

Greene, L.S. and Williams, H.G. (1993) 'Age-related differences in timing control of repetitive movement: application of the Wing-Kristofferson Model, *Research Quarterly for Exercise and Sport*, 64, 32–8.

Jess, M. (2004) *Basic Moves National Training Programme*. Edinburgh: University of Edinburgh.

Kay, P. (2007) *The Sound of Laughter*. London: Arrow Books Ltd. ISBN: 978-0-099505-55-6.

Pankhurst, A. and England Netball (2005) *Preparing for a Life in Sport: A Guide to Good Practice for all People Involved in Netball* leaflet. Leeds: Coachwise Business Solutions/The National Coaching Foundation/England Netball.

Pankhurst, A. and BADMINTON England (2006) *Preparing for a Life in Sport: A Guide to Good Practice for all People Involved in Badminton* leaflet. Leeds: Coachwise Business Solutions/The National Coaching Foundation/ BADMINTON England.

Pankhurst, A. and The British Canoe Union (2006) *Preparing for a Life in Sport: A Guide to Good Practice for all People Involved in Paddlesport* leaflet. Leeds: Coachwise Business Solutions/The National Coaching Foundation/The British Canoe Union.

Pankhurst, A. and British Gymnastics (2006) *Preparing for a Life in Sport: A Guide to Good Practice for all People Involved in Gymnastics* leaflet. Leeds: Coachwise Business Solutions/The National Coaching Foundation/British Gymnastics.

Pankhurst, A. and RFL (2006) *Preparing for a Life in Sport: A Guide to Good Practice for all People Involved in Rugby League* leaflet. Leeds: Coachwise Business Solutions/The National Coaching Foundation/RFL.

Pankhurst, A. and the Amateur Swimming Association (2007) *Preparing for a Life in Sport: A Guide to Good Practice for all People Involved in Swimming* leaflet. Leeds: Coachwise Business Solutions/The National Coaching Foundation/ASA.

Savelsbergh, G., Davids, K., van der Kamp, J. and Bennett, S.J. (eds) (2003) *Development of Movement Coordination in Children: Applications in the Field of Ergonomics, Health Sciences and Sport*. London: Routledge. ISBN: 978-0-415247-37-5.

Sharp, C. (1991) 'The exercise physiology of children', in Grisogono, V. (ed) *Children and Sport: Fitness, Injuries and Diet*. London: John Murray. ISBN: 0-719549-08-6.

Stafford, I and Balyi, I. (2005) *Coaching for Long-term Athlete Development*. Leeds: Coachwise Business Solutions/The National Coaching Foundation. ISBN: 978-1-902523-70-9.

Stevenson, P. (2007) *Including Young Disabled People and SEN Pupils in FUNdamentals and Multi-skill Opportunities*. Loughborough: Youth Sport Trust (unpublished draft document).

Timson-Katchis, M. (2007) 'Coaches, parents and teachers: making the relationship work', *coaching edge*, 9: 16–17.

Whitehead, J. (1993) 'Why Children choose to do sport – or stop', in Lee, M. (ed) *Coaching Children in Sport: Principles and Practice*. London: Routledge. ISBN: 978-0-419182-50-4.

Williams, H., Woollacott, M. and Ivry, R. (1992) 'Timing and motor control in clumsy children', *Journal of Motor Behavior*, 24, 165–72.

Workshops

Multi-skill Club Workshop

FUNdamentals of Agility

FUNdamentals of Balance

FUNdamentals of Coordination

Multi-skills Inclusion

To book a workshop, contact the sports coach UK Workshop Booking Centre.

Tel: 0845-601 3054

Email: scukworkshops@sportscoachuk.org

Mission Statement

sports coach UK is dedicated to guiding the development and implementation of a coaching system, recognised as a world leader, for all coaches at every level in the UK.

We will work with our partners to achieve this, by promoting:

- professional and ethical values
- inclusive and equitable practice
- agreed national standards of competence as a benchmark at all levels
- a regulated and licensed structure
- recognition, value and appropriate funding and reward
- a culture and structure of innovation, constant renewal and continuous professional development (CPD).